Introduction

Before reading the content in this book which hypothesizes that interest rates can be set by observing Mars, while presuming that the movements of the planet Mars around the sun has influence on investor behavior, it is important to take into account a recent study published in Nature Communications in March of 2024, roughly 5 years after this idea was first introduced to the public. In that study published in March of 2024, researchers discovered that Mars is exerting a gravitation pull on earth's tilt, exposing earth to warmer temperatures and more sunlight, all within a 2.4 million year cycle. I assert that this allows us to surmise that, even within smaller timeframes, Mars is still exerting a gravitational pull on earth's axial tilt, enough to raise temperatures when the planet is within 30 degrees of the lunar node, which would affect human behavior. Citing the fact of numerous studies that link aggression and irritability to warmer temperatures, I establish an axiom and then assert that Mars within 30 degrees of the lunar node should affect the brain by reducing cognition and compelling aggression and irritability.

Here is a visual of what is happening as Mars travels around the sun and exerts a gravitational pull on Earth axial tilt. In this first graphic, Mars gravity is pulling earth's tilt away from the sun.

In this next graphic, Mars's gravity is pulling Earth's tilt toward the sun.

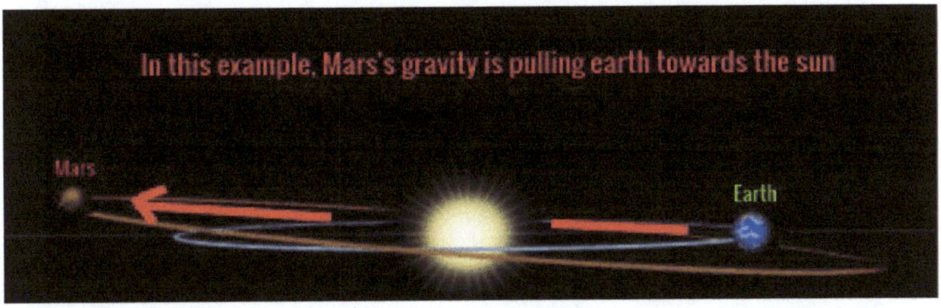

In this latter visual, this scenario should have the most prominent effect on human behavior. Here is how this scenario of Mars pulling earth's tilt towards the sun appears in an astrology chart. This is the chart for the October 29, 1929 Stock market crash. Planet earth is always opposite the sun in an astrology chart.

−12.82%

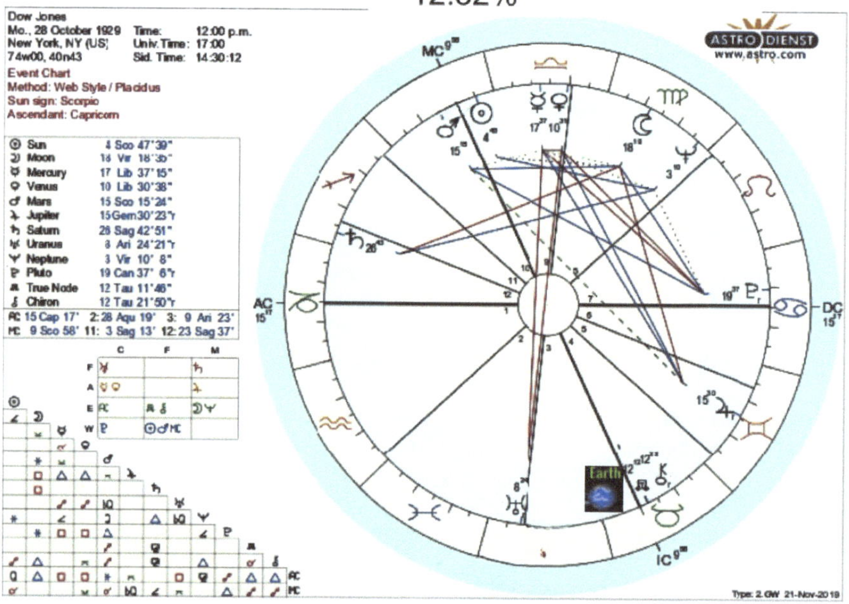

Here is the view from above of the same planetary configuration scenario.

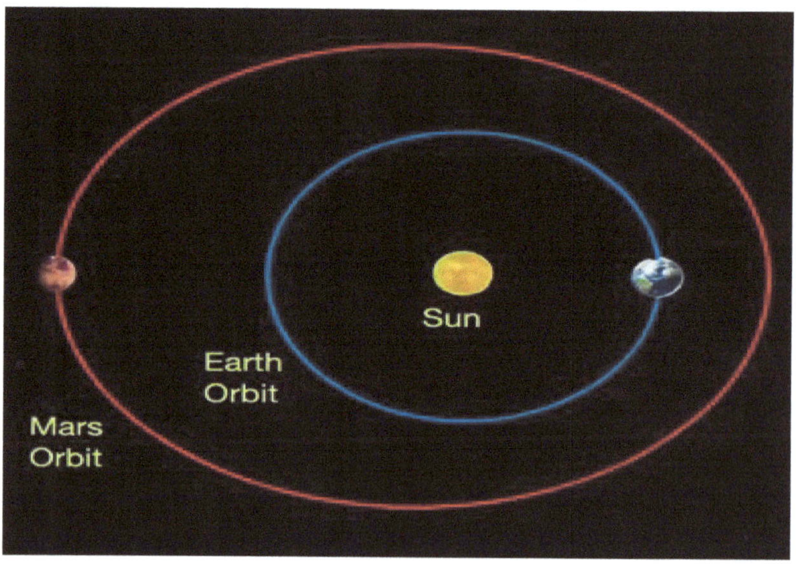

In all the major stock market crashes and one-day drops, Mars was somewhere along the white line as shown in this graphic, which according to

the research, would indicate that Mars is pulling the earth's tilt towards the sun, triggering irritability

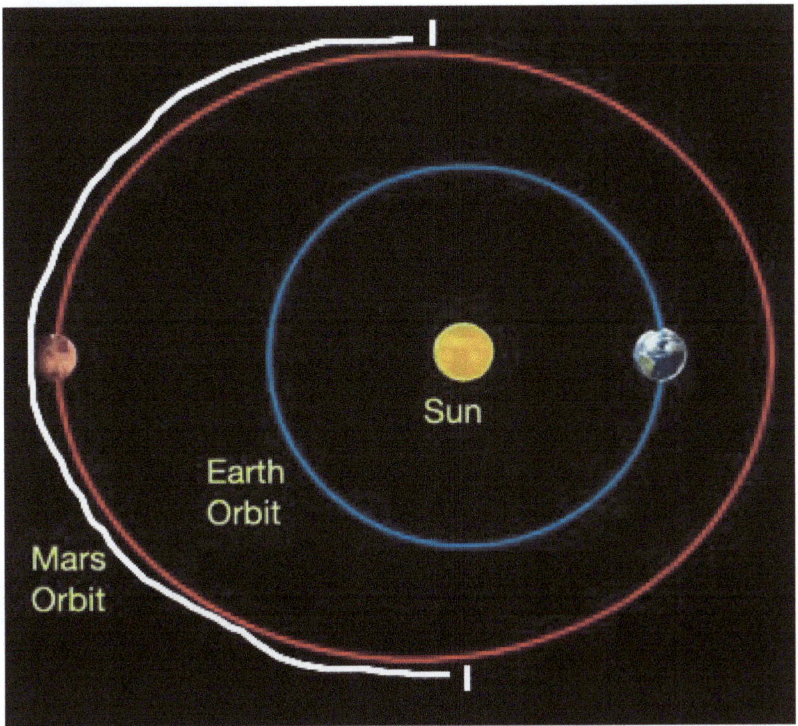

Here is how this same visual is represented in an astrology chart. See the next page Notice the white line.

−12.82%

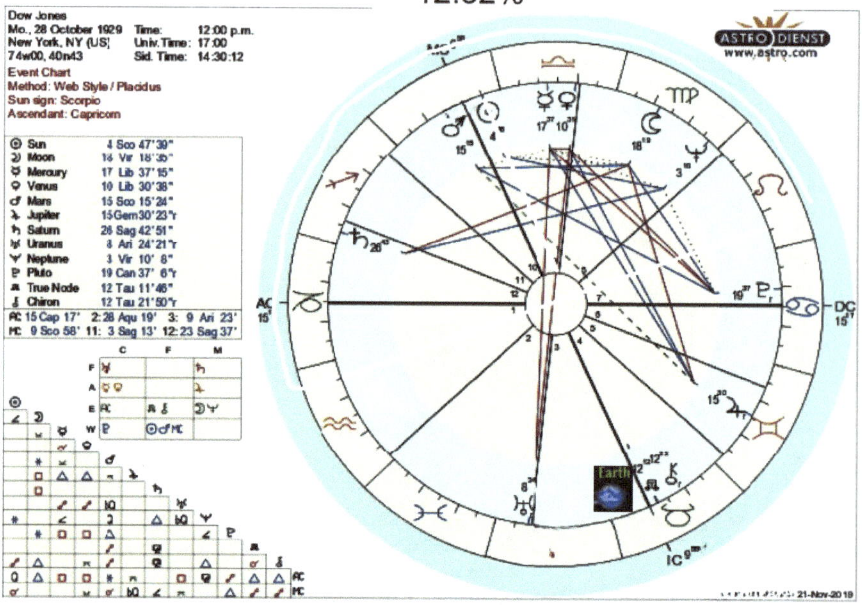

All the highest one day stock market crashes or one-day drops occurred when Mars appeared within that white line, as drawn out from the degree of the sun.

This perspective should help the reader move beyond the preconceived notion of absurdity and realize that this has scientific merit

Here are the 25 major stock market crashes and downturns in US history. The data shows a 100% correlation between such events and Mars position in relation to earth. Every stock market crash and major stock downturn in US history has happened when Mars was orbiting behind the sun from earth's point of view.

The dates of each stock market crash are mapped with astrology charts and a graphics representing Mars position in space at the time of the crash.

October 19, 1987 Stock market crash

−22.61%

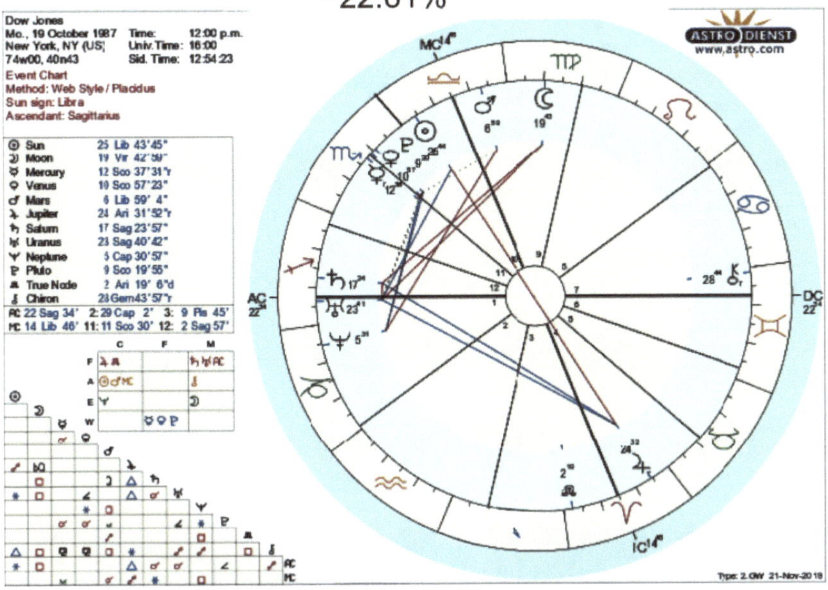

Here is how Mars was positioned in space that day relative to earth

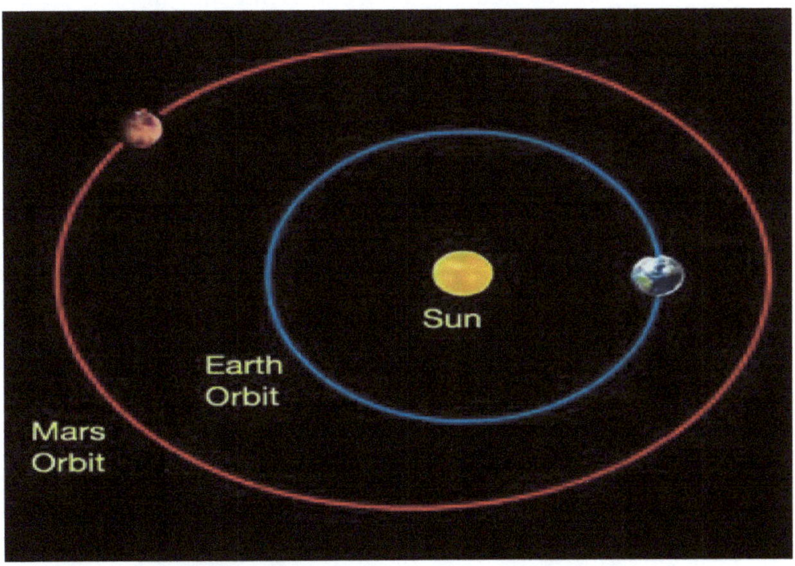

November 6 1929 Stock Market Crash

−9.92%

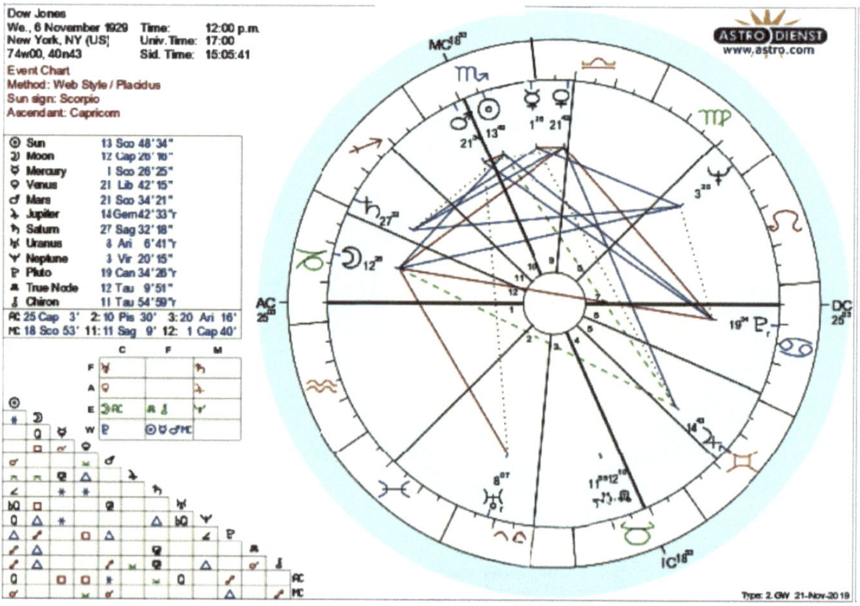

Here is where Mars was located in space from earth's point of view

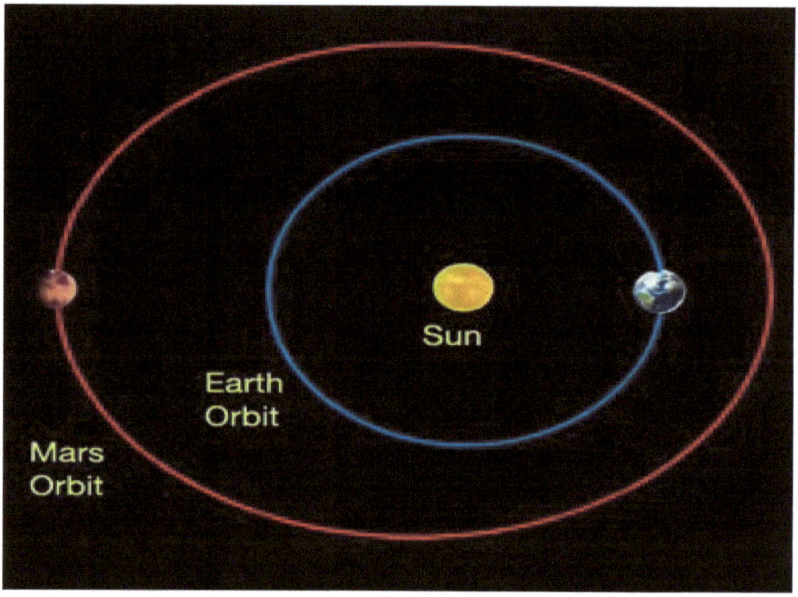

March 16, 2020 Stock Market crash

-12.93

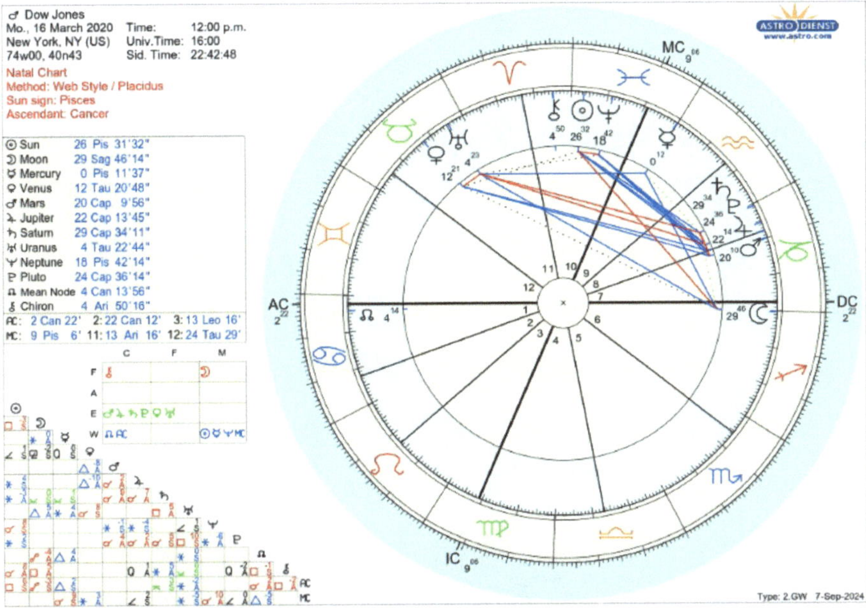

Here is how Mars was positioned in the sky relative to earth

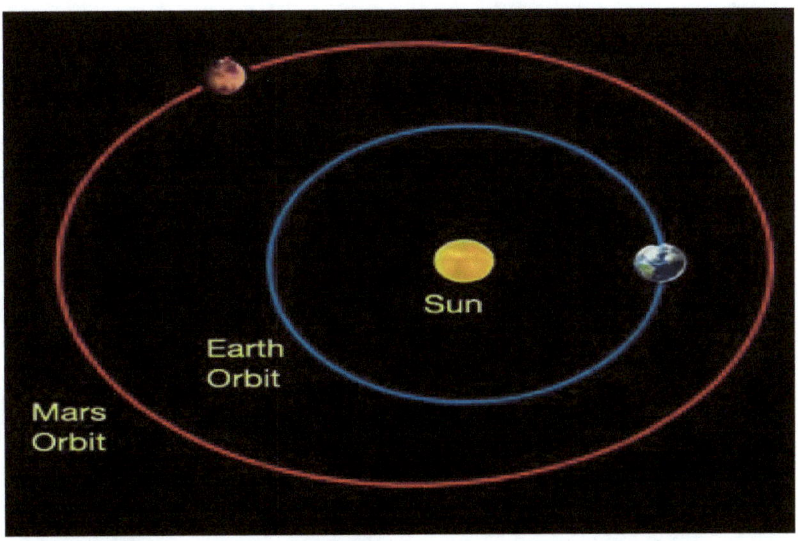

March 12, 2020 Stock Market Crash

-9.99

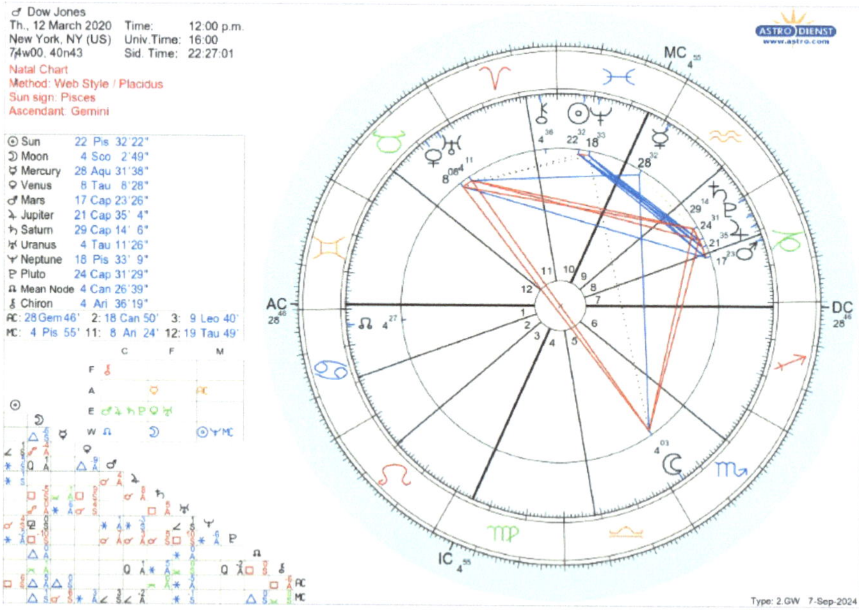

Here is how Mars was positioned in the sky on that day

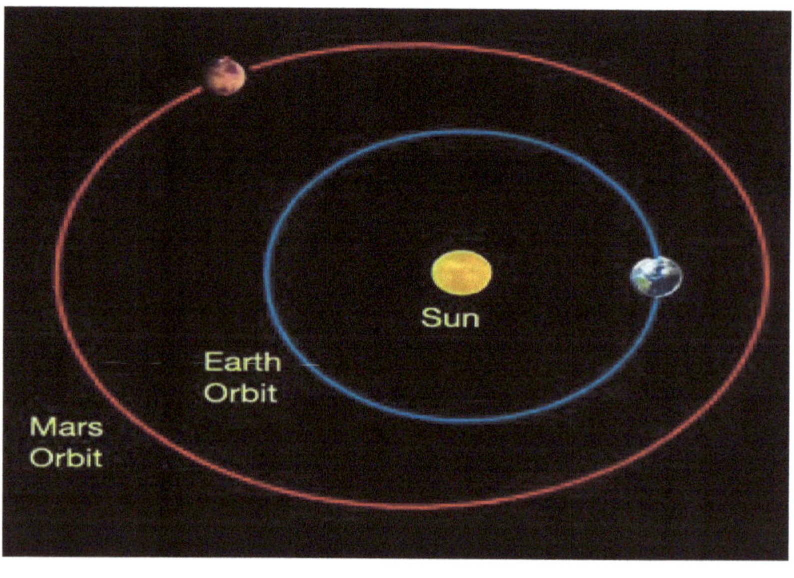

March 9, 2020 Stock Market Crash

-7.79

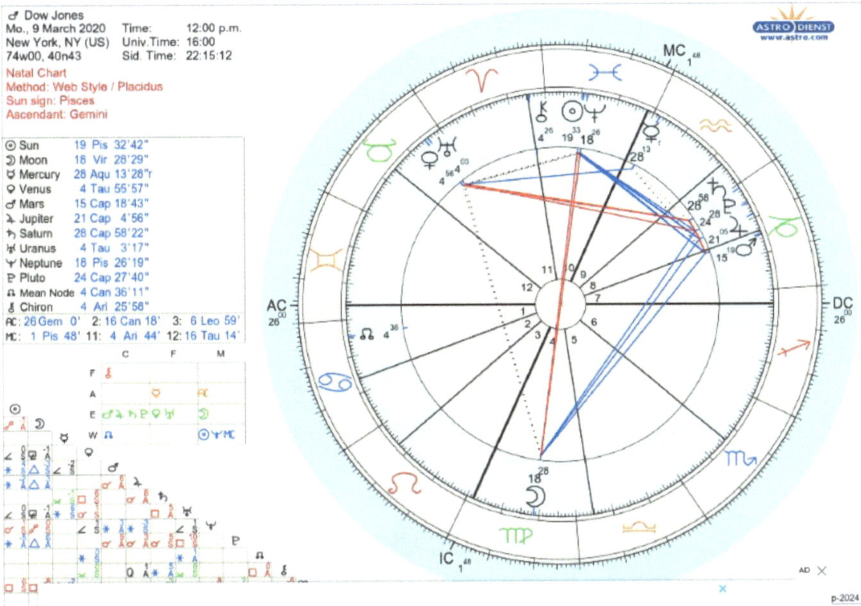

Here is where Mars was in the sky that day

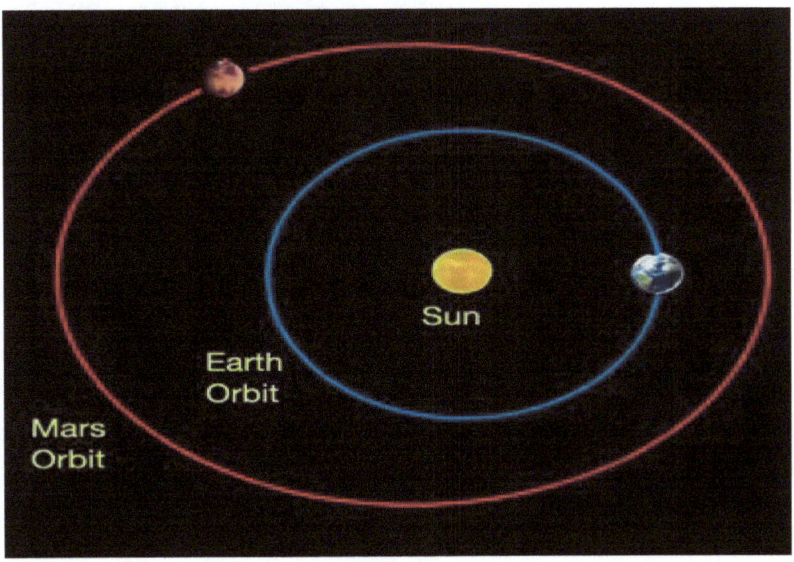

December 18, 1899, the stock market dropped -8.72 percent

−8.72 %

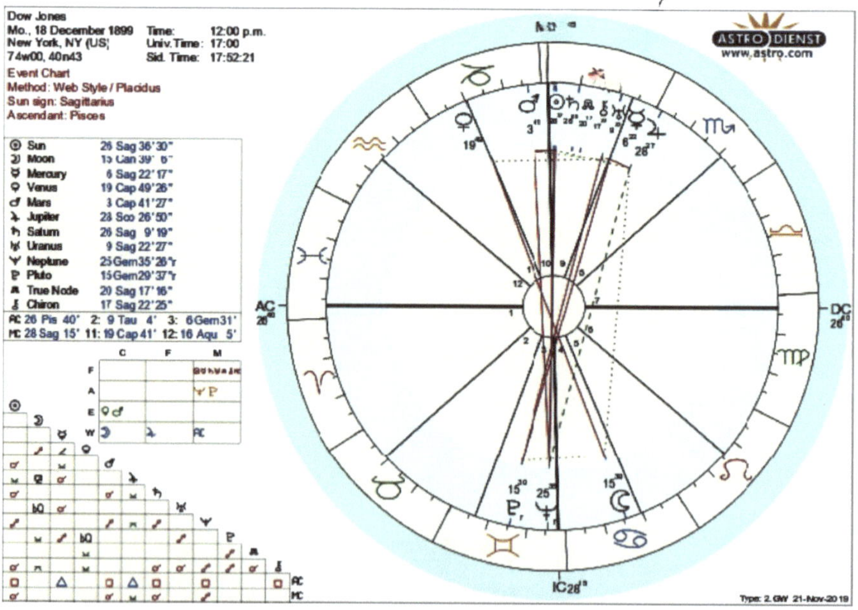

Here is how Mars lined up in the sky that day

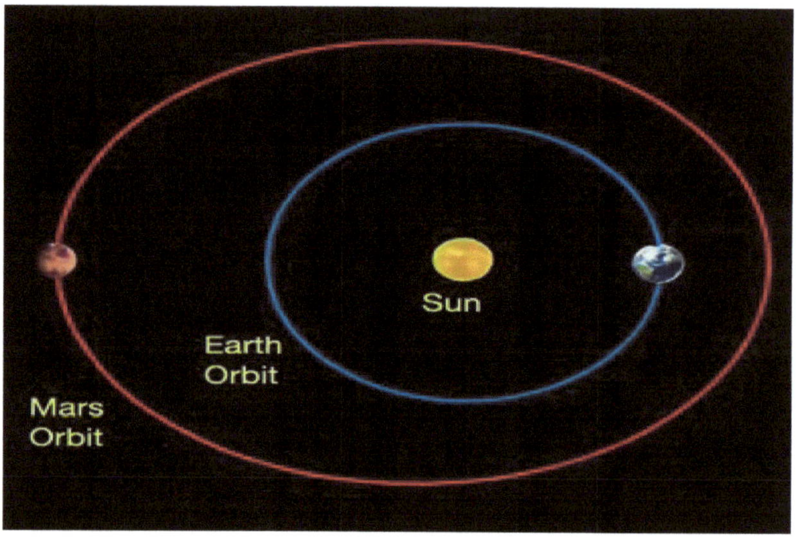

August 12, 1932, stock market dropped -8.4 %

-8.40 %

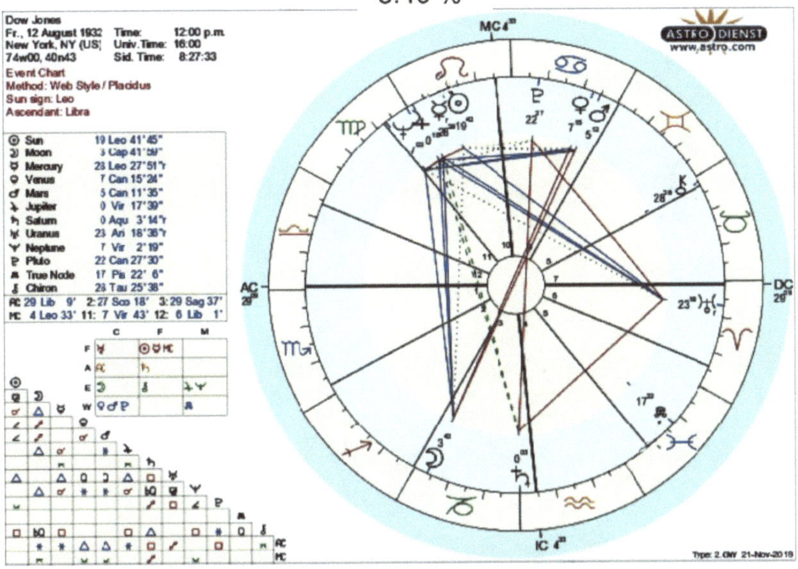

Here is how Mars was positioned in the sky that day

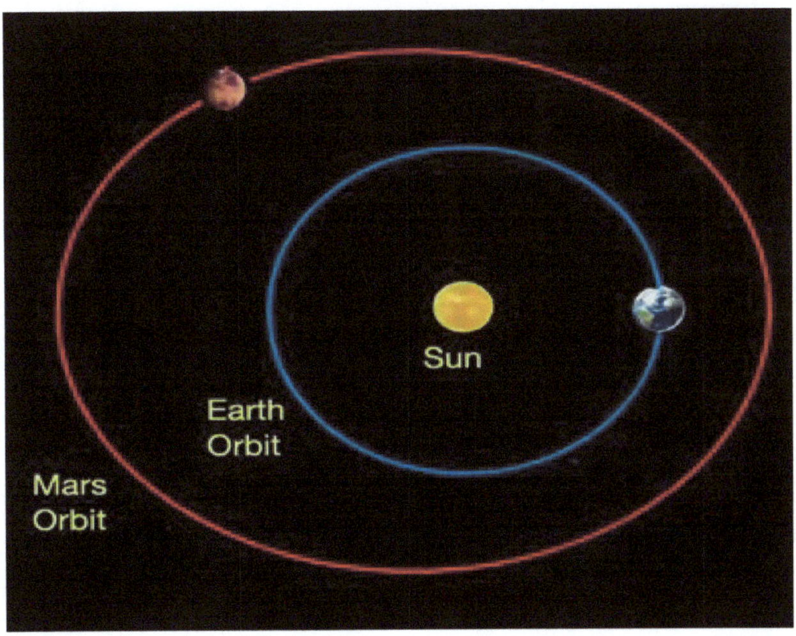

March 14, 1907, the stock market fell -8.29%

-8.29%

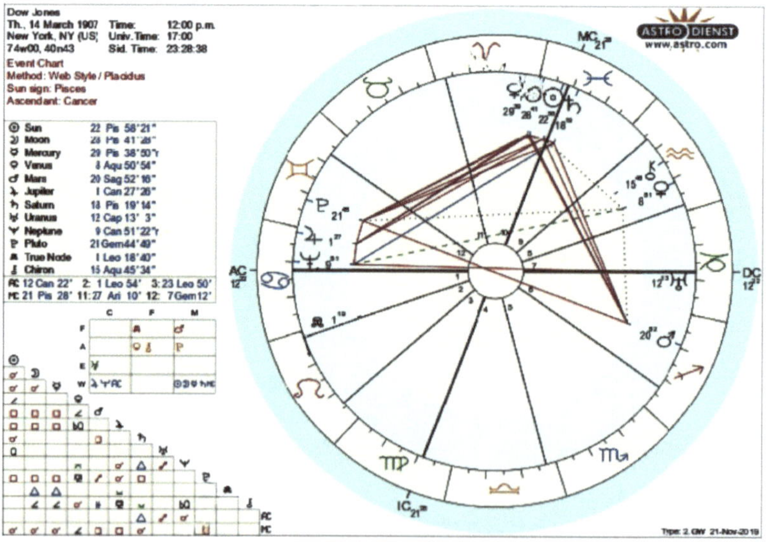

Here is how Mars was positioned in the sky that day

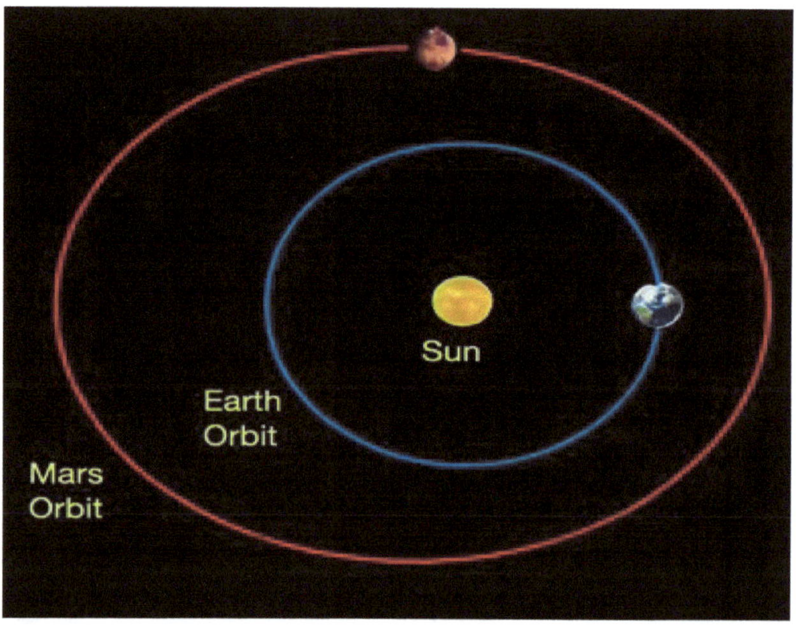

October 26, 1987, the stock market dropped -8.04%

−8.04

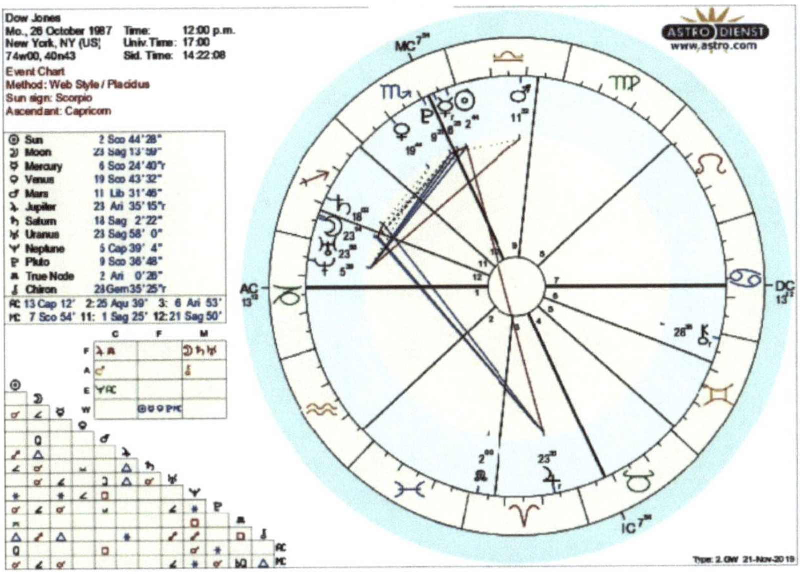

Here is where Mars was positioned in the sky that day

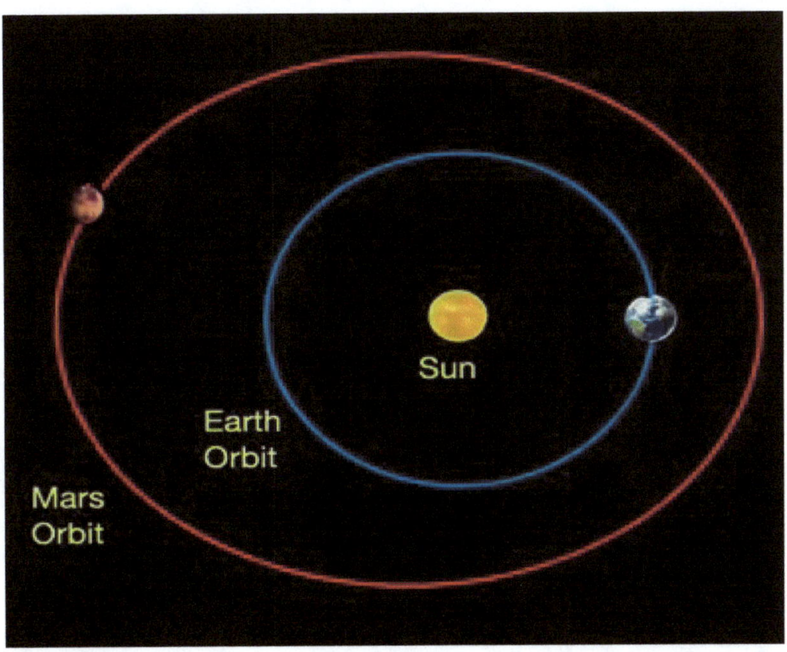

October 15, 2008, the stock market fell -7.87%

-7.87%

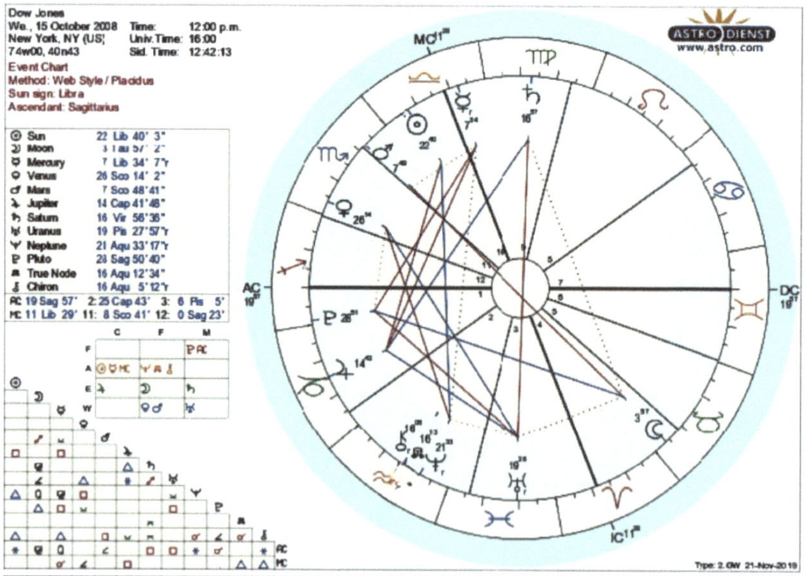

Here is where Mars was positioned in the sky that day

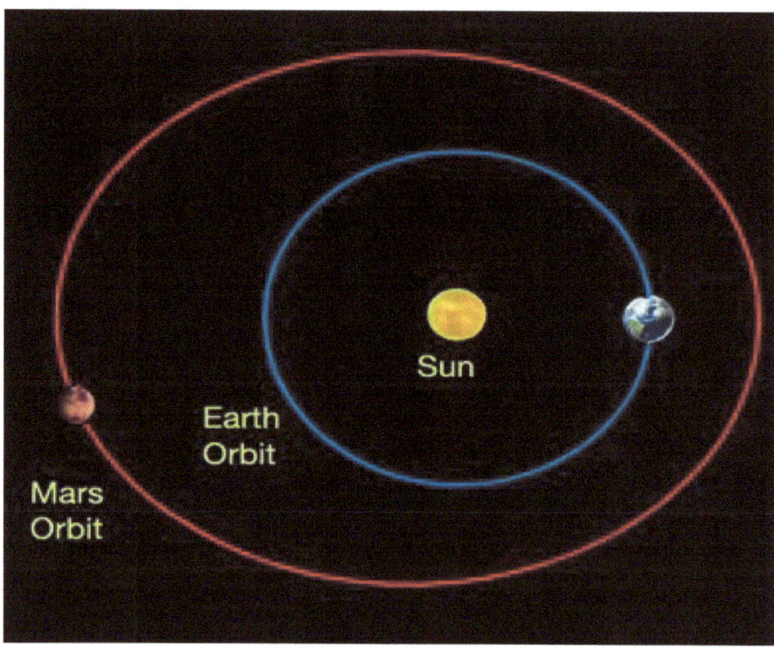

July 21, 1933, The stock market dropped -7.84

-7.84%

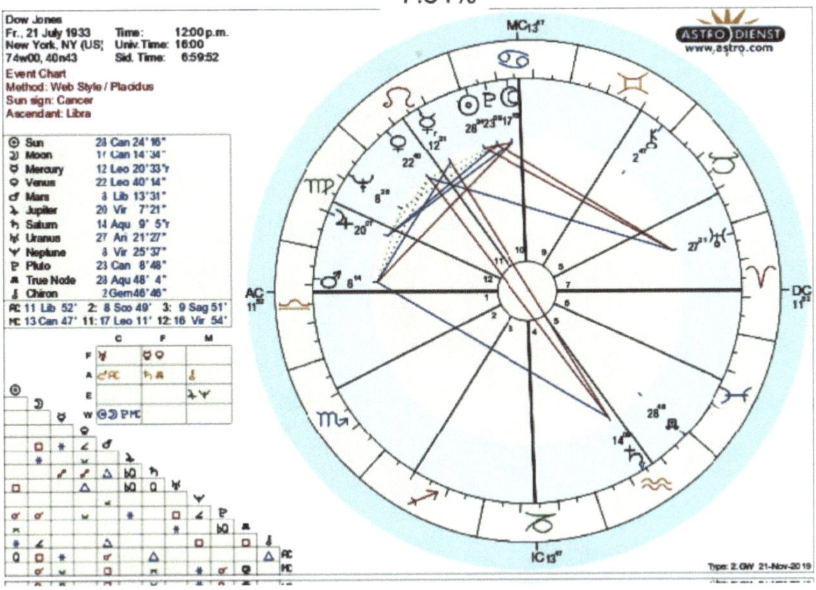

Here is where Mars was positioned in the sky that day

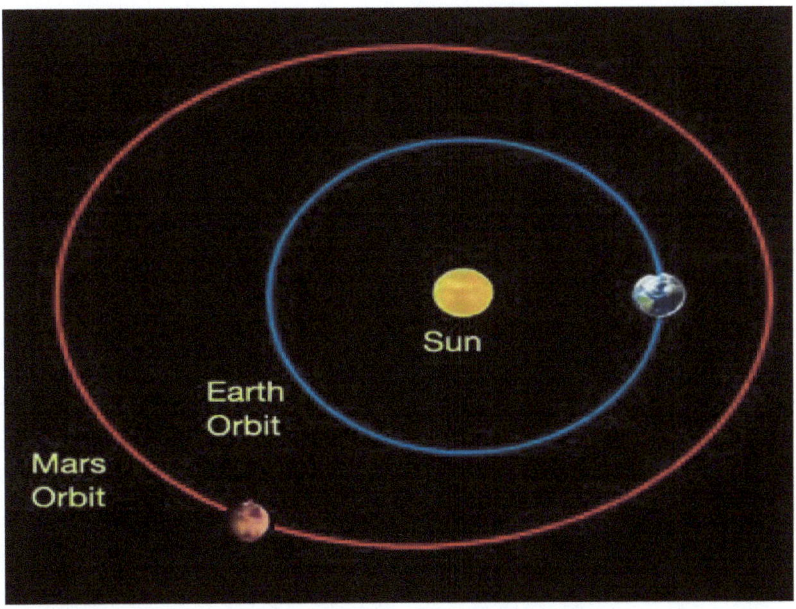

October 18, 1937, the stock market dropped -7.75%

-7.75%

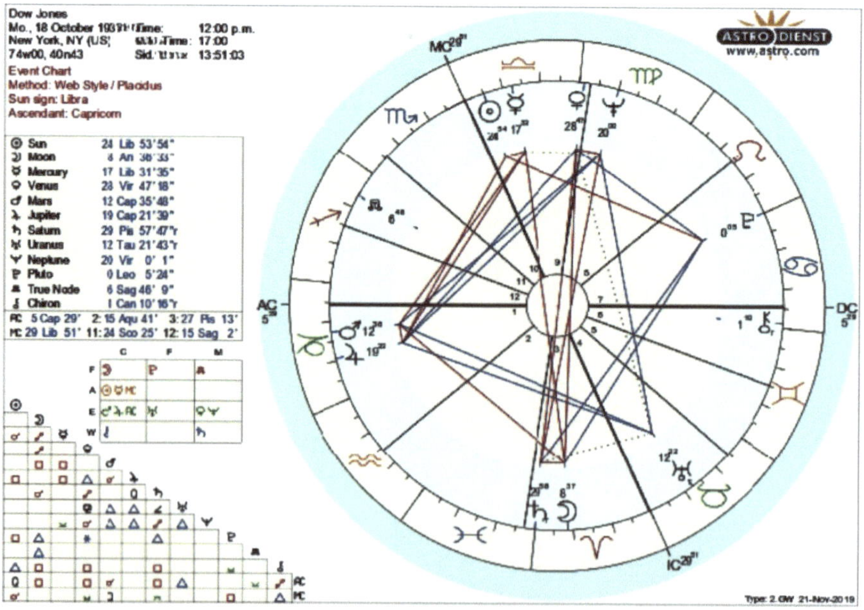

Here is where Mars was positioned on that day

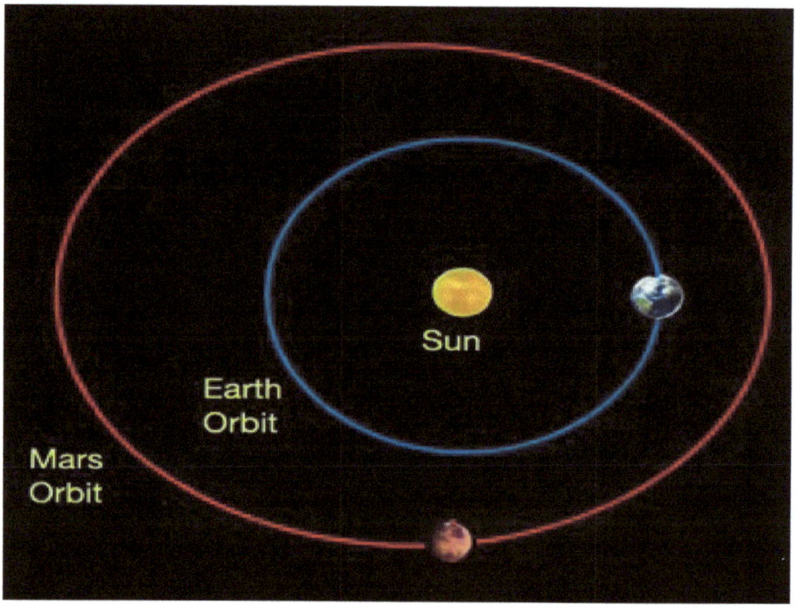

On December 1, 2008, the stock market dropped -7.70%

-7.70%

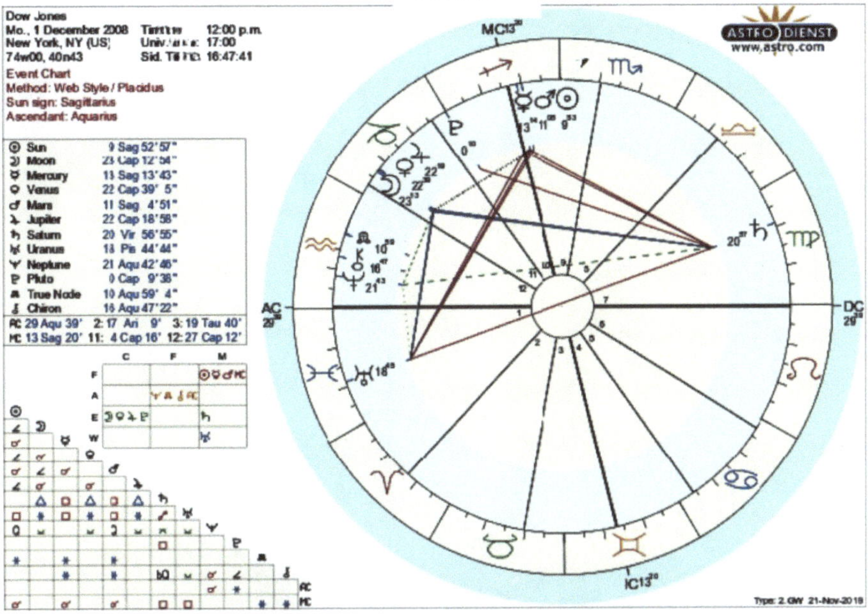

Here is where Mars was positioned in that sky that day

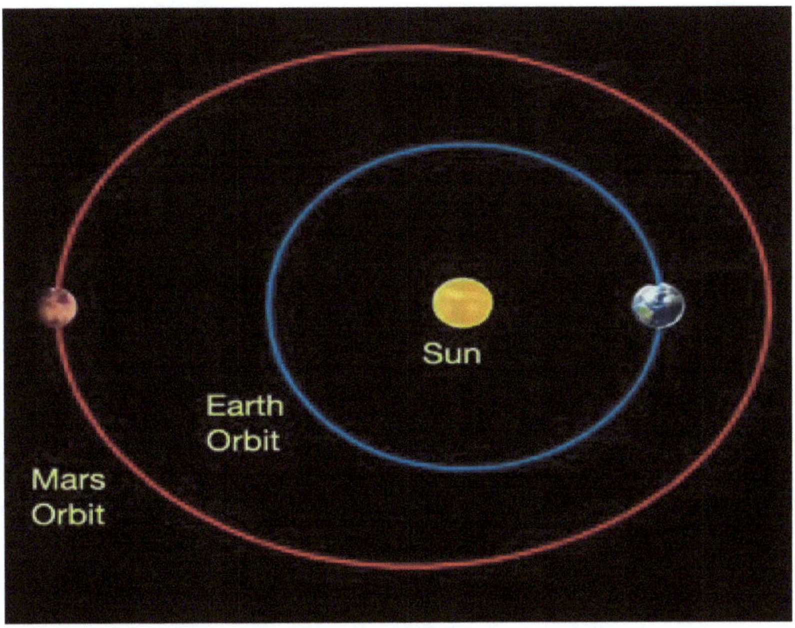

October 9, 2008, the stock market fell -7.33%

-7.33 %

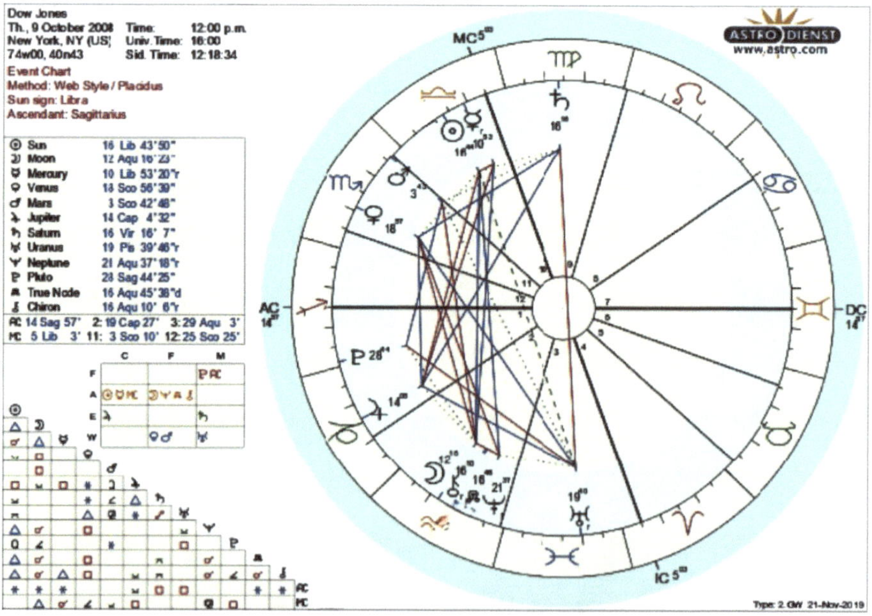

Here is where mars was positioned in the sky on that day

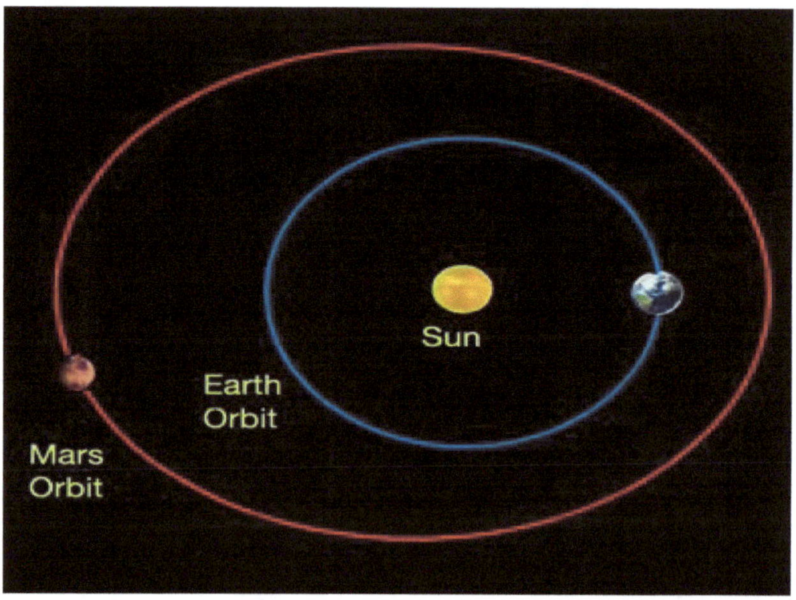

On February 1, 1917, the stock market dropped -7.24%

-7.24%

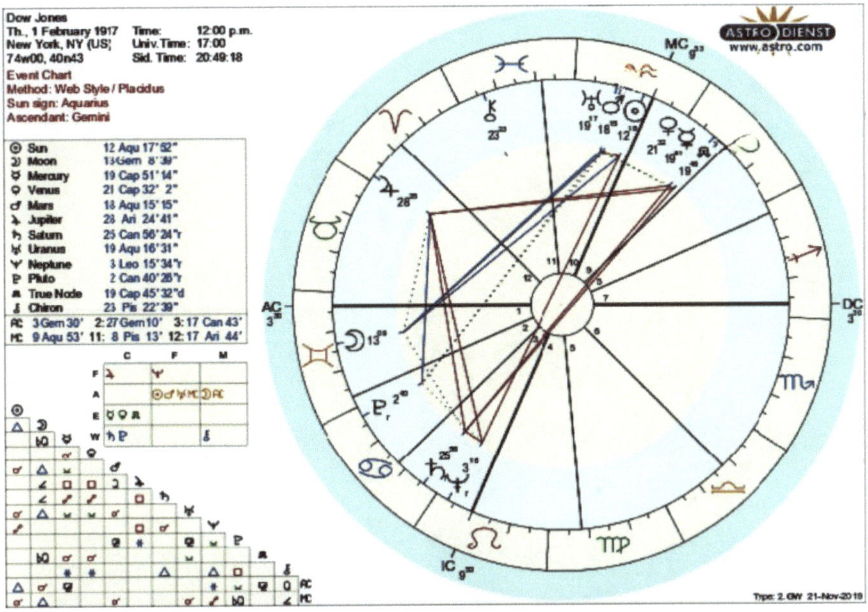

Here is where Mars was positioned in the sky on that day

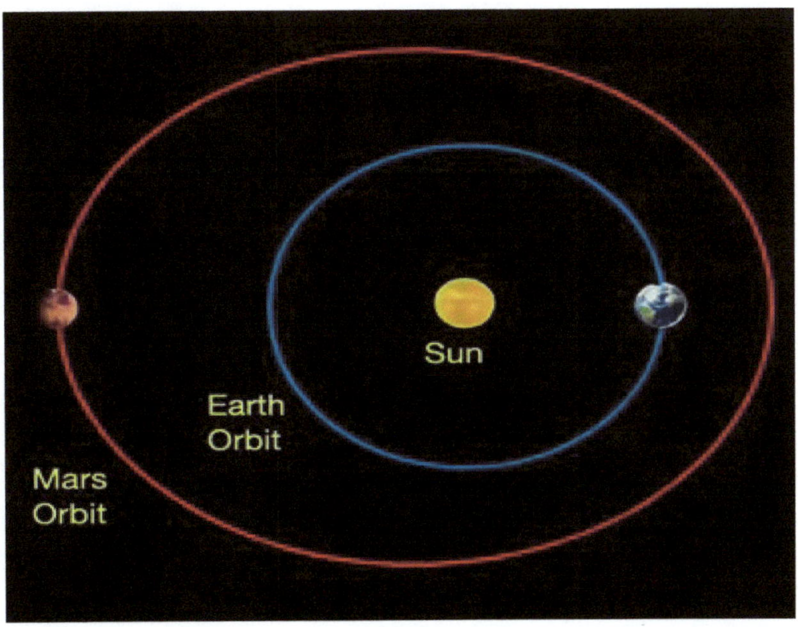

On October 27, 1997, the stock market crashed -7.18%

−7.18%

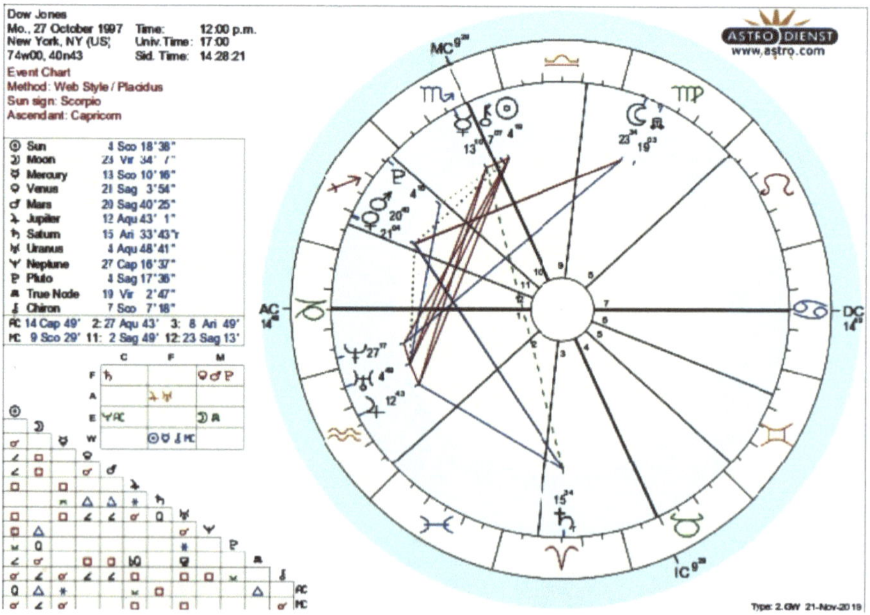

Here is where Mars was positioned in the sky on that day

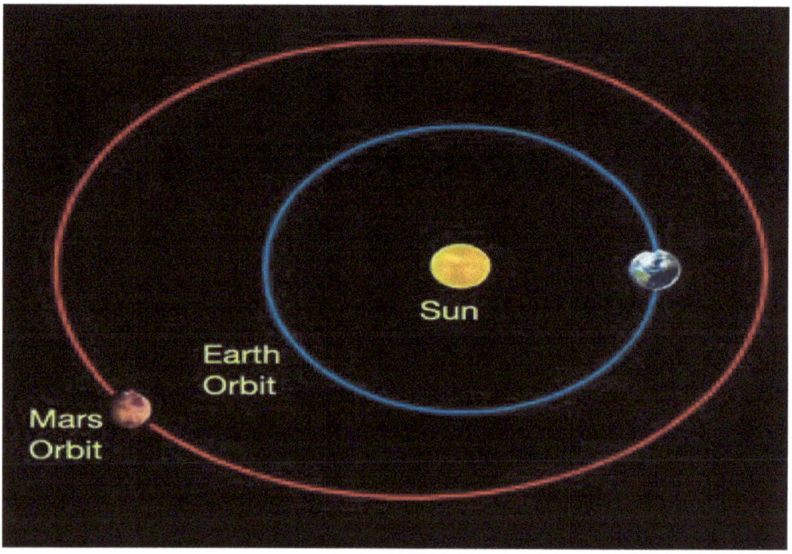

October 5, 1932, the stock market dropped -7.15 percent

−7.15 %

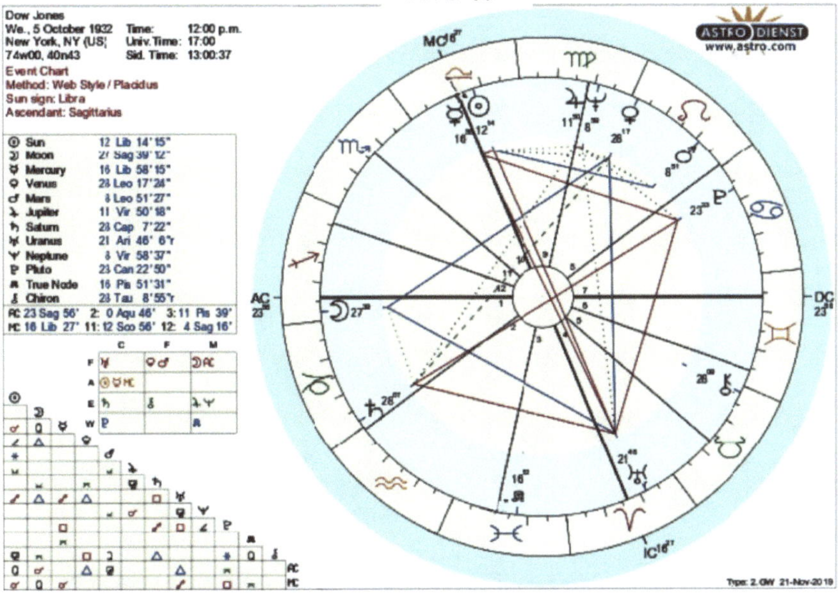

Here is where Mars was positioned in the sky on that day

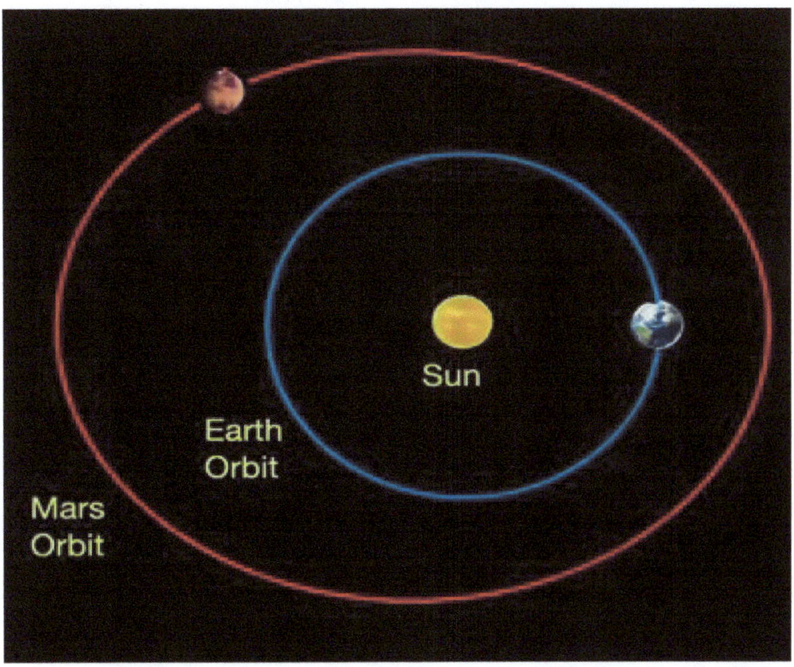

September 17, 2001, the stock market fell -7.13%

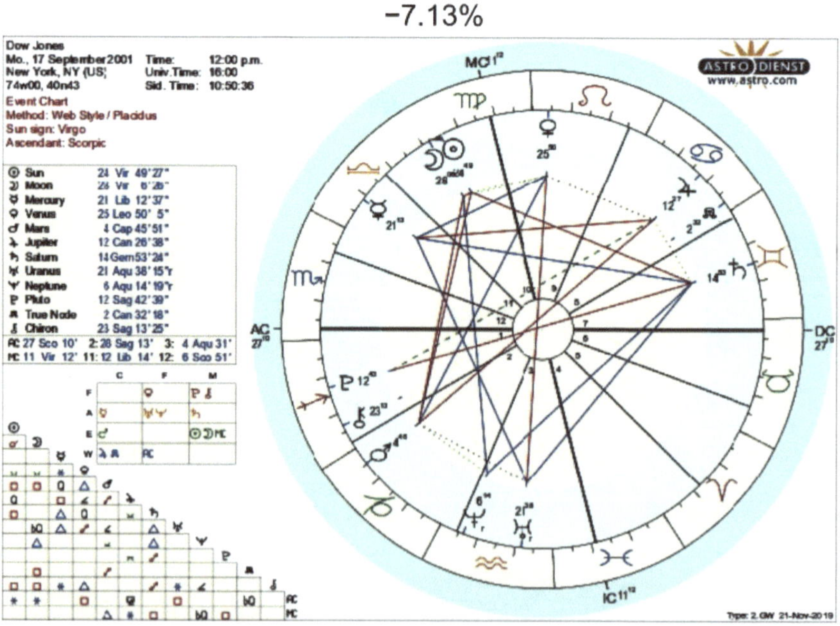

Here is where Mars was positioned in the sky that day

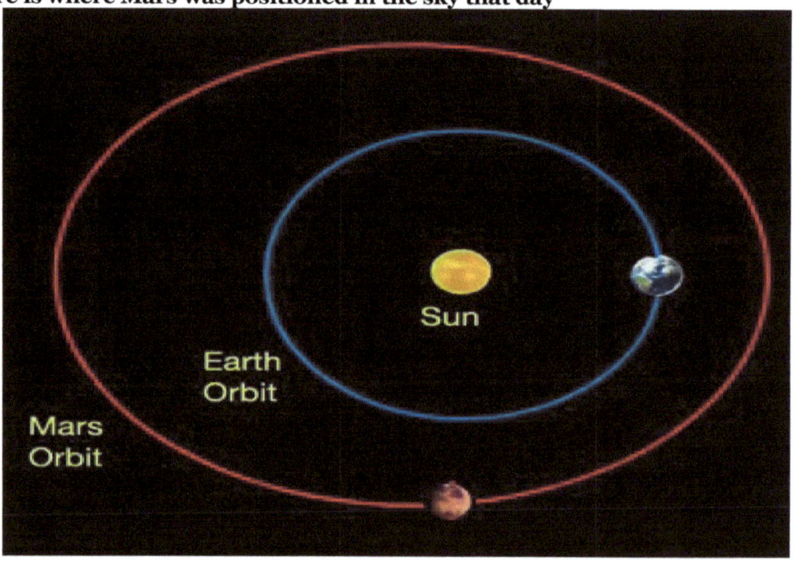

September 24, 1931, the stock market dropped -7.07%

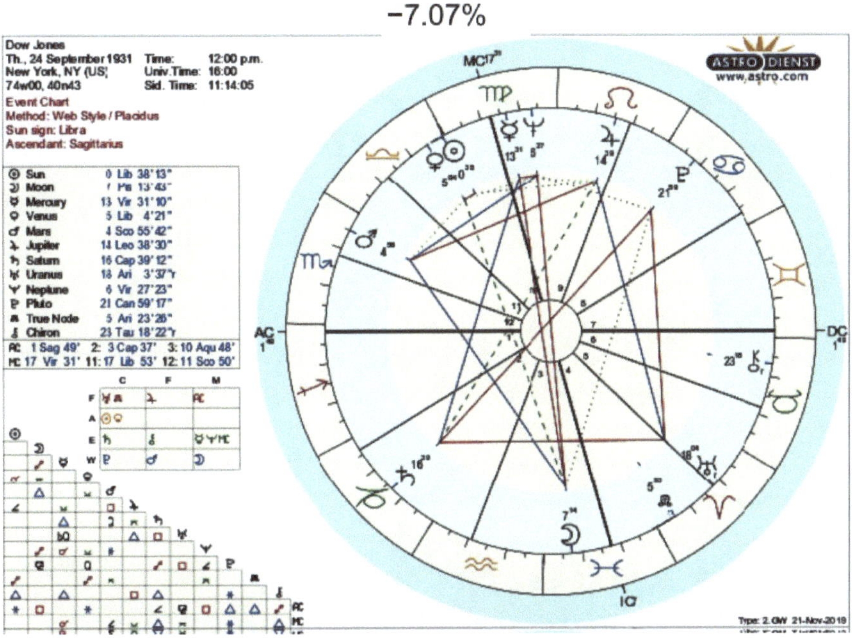

Here is where Mars was positioned in the sky on that day

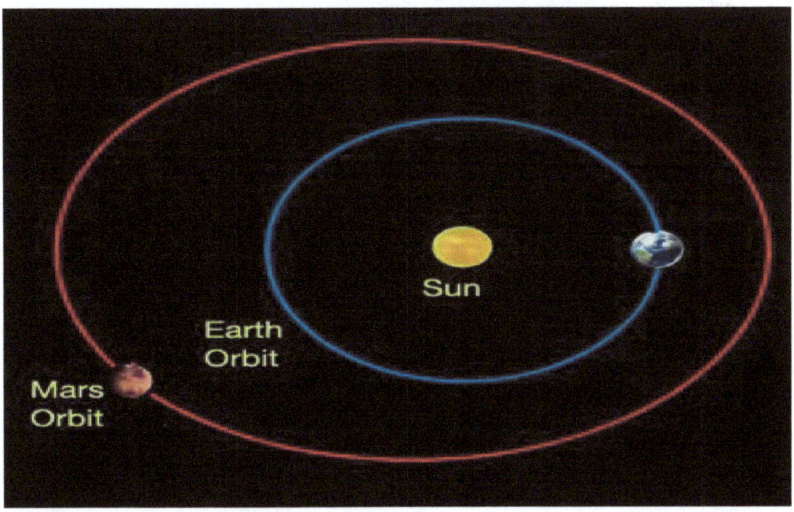

July 20, 1932, the stock market dropped -7.07%

-7.07%

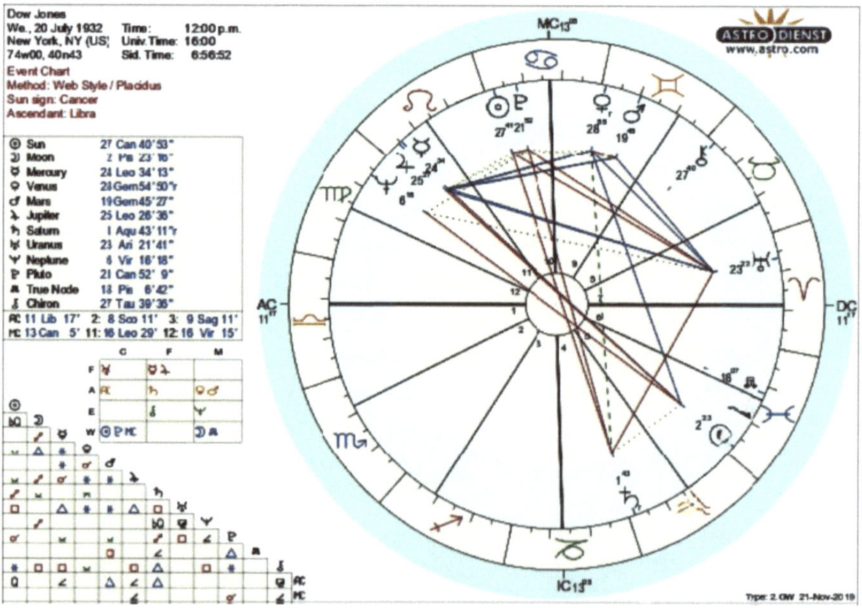

Here is where Mars was positioned in the sky that day

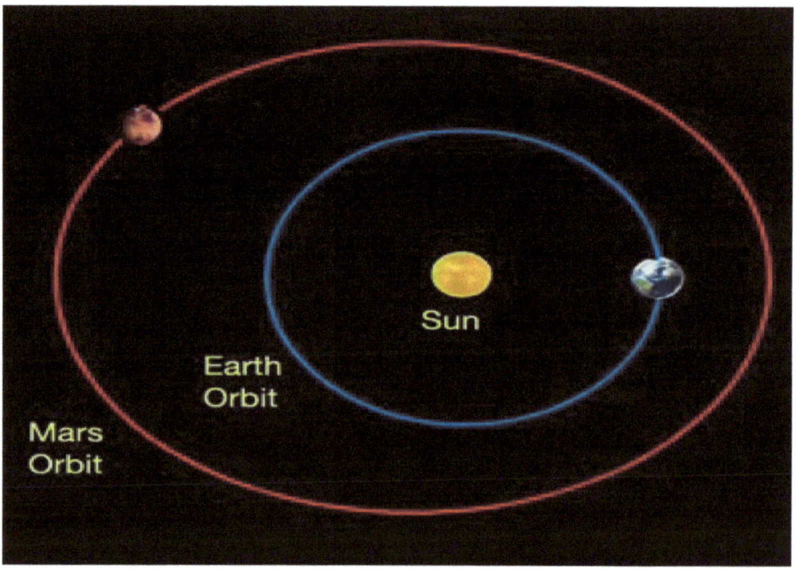

July 30, 1914, the stock market dropped -6.91%

−6.91%

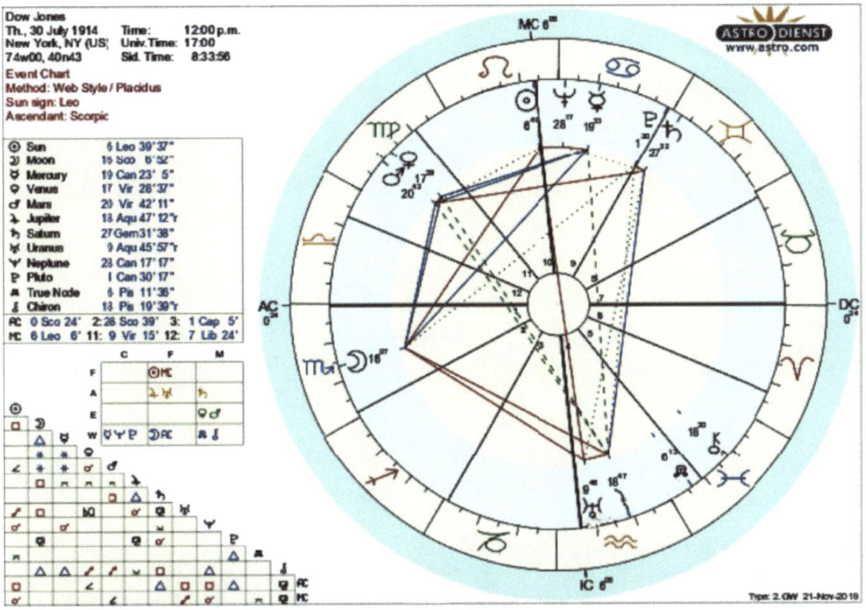

Here is where Mars was positioned in the sky on that day

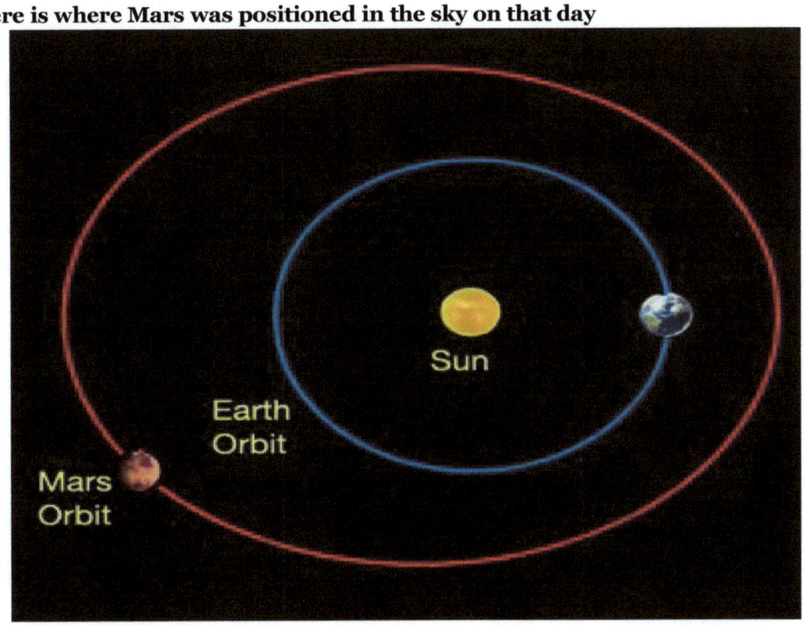

September 29, 2008, the stock market dropped – 6.98%

-6.98%

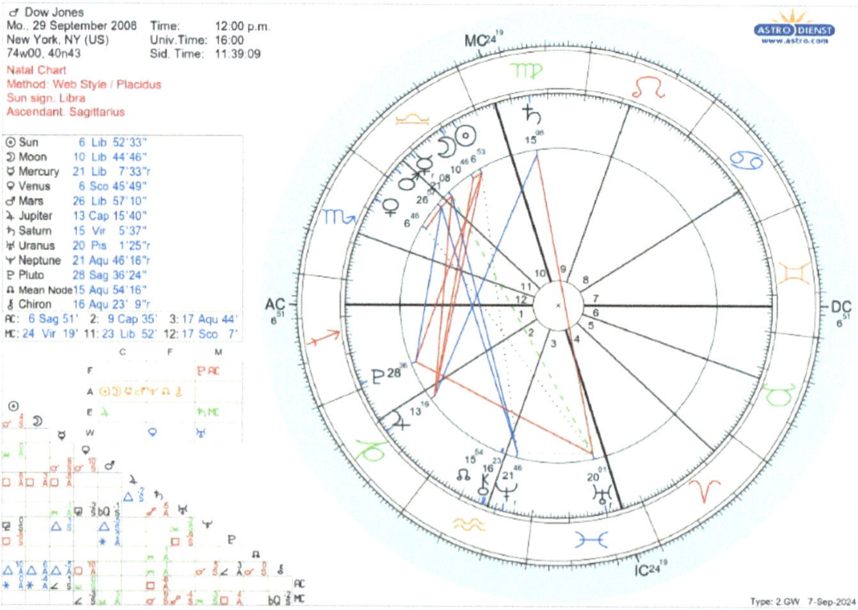

Here is where Mars was positioned in the sky that day

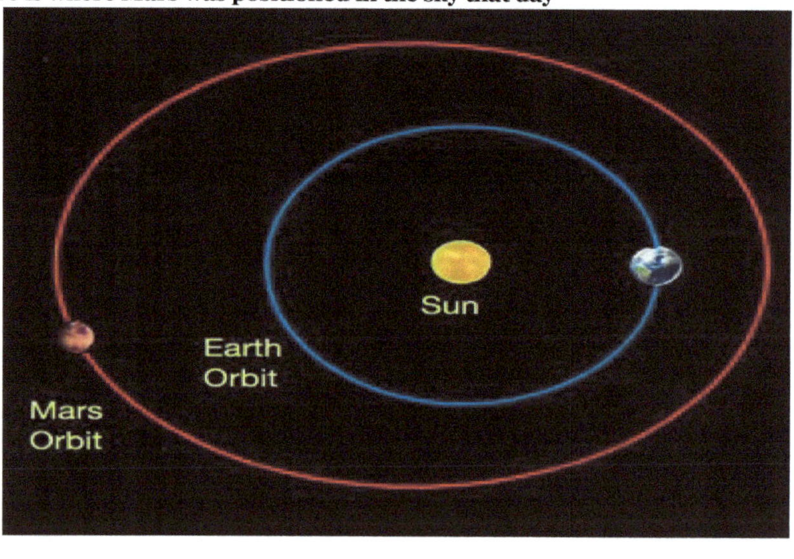

August 8, 2011, the stock market dropped -5.15%

-5.15%

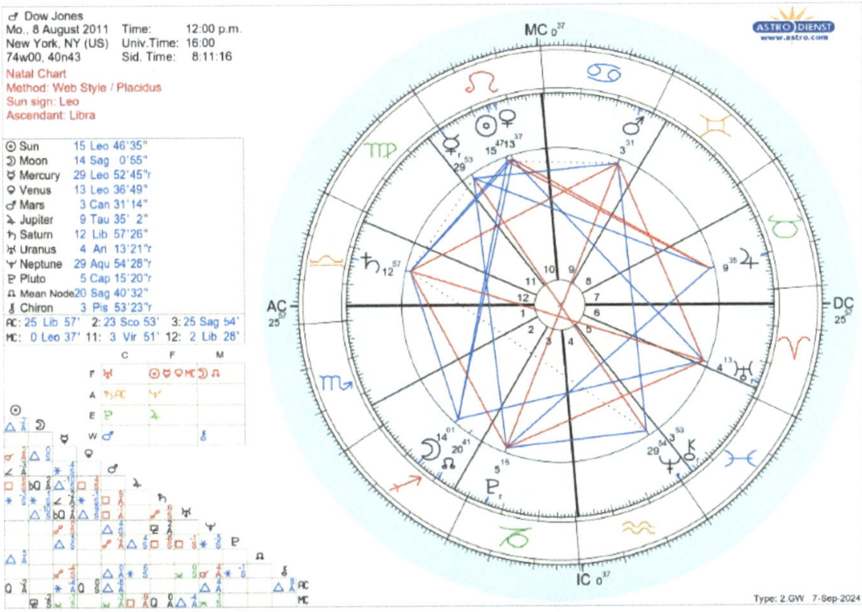

Here is where Mars was positioned in the sky on that day

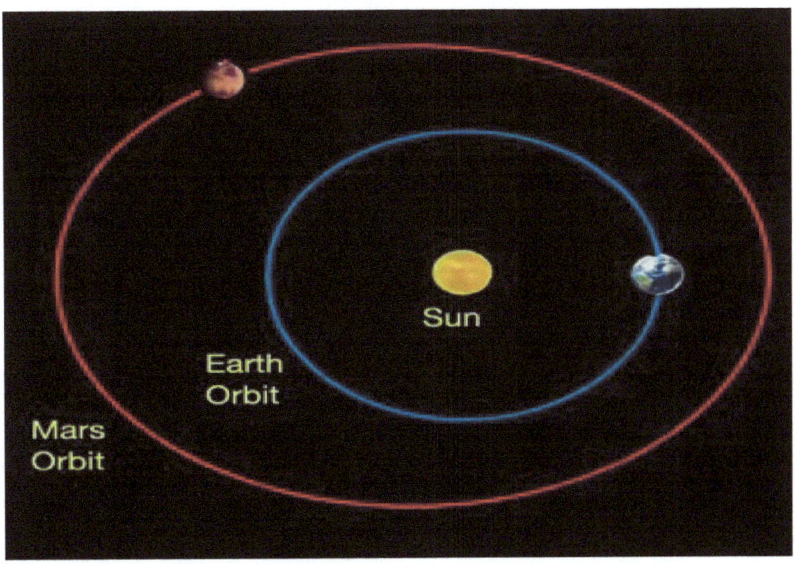

April 14, 2000, the stock market dropped -5.66%

-5.66%

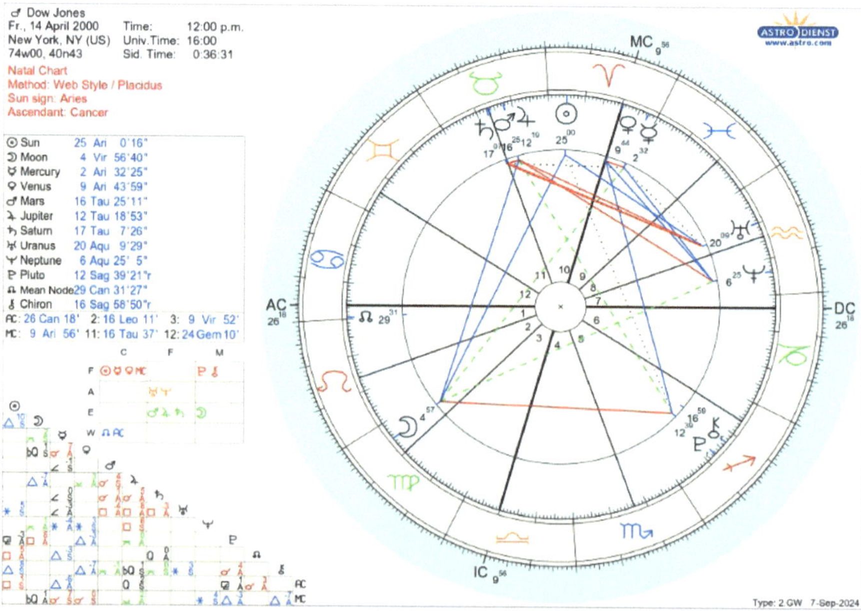

Here is where Mars was positioned in the sky that day

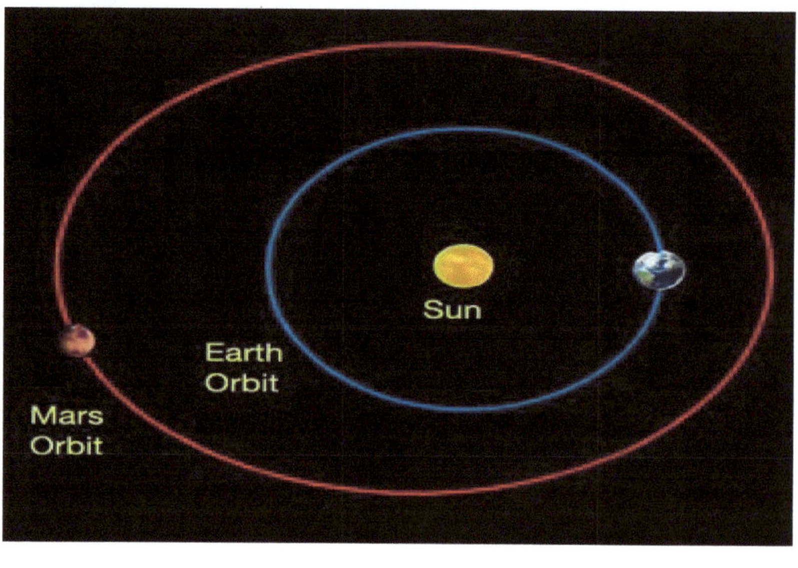

In all the days of major stock market crashes and downturns in the Dow Jones history, Mars was always in the orbital phase, from earth's point of view, marked with the white line.

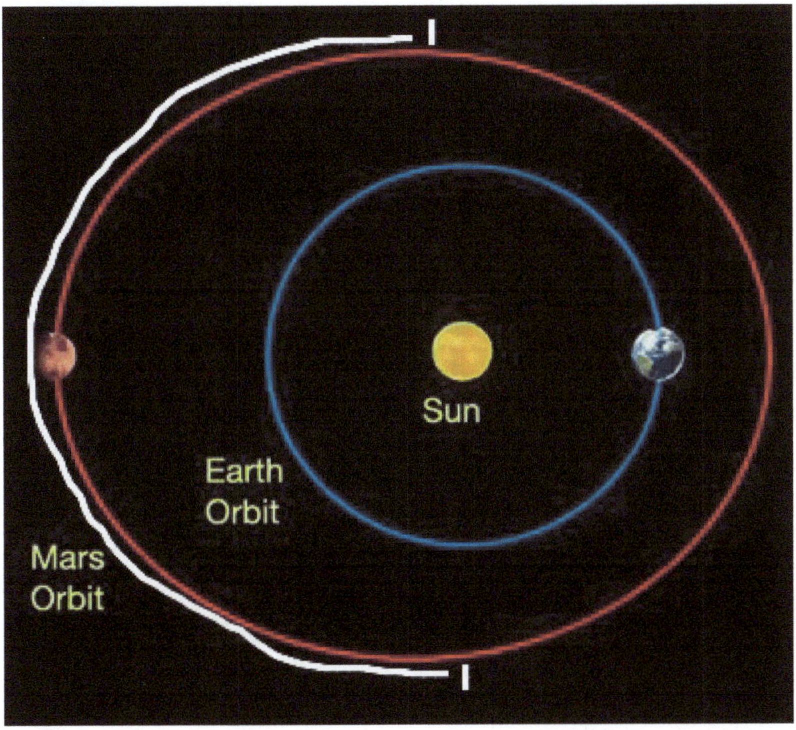

This data shows that a major stock market crash will never happen when Mars is orbiting in the area not marked with the white line. We can say this with 100% certainty.

The white area is the phase of the orbit when Mars is going further out from earth, but also when it's gravity is puling Earth's axial tilt towards the sun, possibly bringing warmer temperatures, which should affect investor sentiment most negatively, presuming that warmer temperatures relative to the mean affect cognitive function and trigger some variant of irritability or pessimism. There are studies that corroborate this dynamic between warmer temperatures and negative mood states.

Outside of the white area, as Mars gets closer to earth, Mars's gravity is puling earth's axial tilt away from the sun, bring presumably cooler temperatures, and less negative mood outcomes, which may explain why major stock market crashes never happen during that phase of Mars's orbit

Hypothesis that the Federal Reserve can set interest rates based on the movements of the planet Mars and the timing of the Jewish Shmita year

Anthony of Boston

Hypothesis that the Federal Reserve can set interest rates based on the movements of the planet Mars and the timing of the Jewish Shmita year

Data going back to 1896 shows that as of April 2020, percentage-wise, the Dow Jones rose 857%. When Mars was within 30 degrees of the lunar node since 1896, the Dow rose 136%. When Mars was not within 30 degrees of the lunar node, the Dow rose 721%. Mars retrograde phases during the time Mars was within 30 degrees of the lunar node was not counted in that data as Mars being within 30 degrees of the lunar node. I'm hypothesizing that the Federal Reserve can set interest rates based on the movements of the planet Mars. Here is an overview comparison of the actual Dow Jones annual percentage returns versus the Dow Jones annual percentage returns that exclude the days that Mars was within 30 degrees of the lunar node.

Date	DOW Yearly Percent Return	DOW Yearly % Return without including the days that Mars was within 30 degrees of the lunar node	Date	DOW Yearly Percent Return	DOW Yearly % Return without including the days that Mars was within 30 degrees of the lunar node
12/31/19	+22.34	+17.83	12/31/86	+22.58	+18.80
12/31/18	-5.63	-0.60	12/31/85	+27.66	+17.39
12/31/17	+25.08	+14.94	12/31/84	-3.74	-3.49
12/31/16	+13.42	+9.17	12/31/83	+20.27	+22.90
12/31/15	-2.23	-12.16	12/31/82	+19.61	+9.99
12/31/14	+7.52	+6.08	12/31/81	-9.23	+5.85
12/31/13	+26.50	+19.95	12/31/80	+14.93	-1.99
12/31/12	+7.26	+10.18	12/31/79	+4.19	+6.70
12/31/11	+5.53	+8.45	12/31/78	-3.15	-8.18
12/31/10	+11.02	+5.49	12/31/77	-17.27	-15.74
12/31/09	+18.82	+26.21	12/31/76	+17.86	+17.78
12/31/08	-33.84	-21.66	12/31/75	+38.32	+26.85
12/31/07	+6.43	-3.56	12/31/74	-27.57	-18.20
12/31/06	+16.29	+7.30	12/31/73	-16.58	-11.20
12/31/05	-0.61	-0.51	12/31/72	+14.58	+11.05
12/31/04	+3.15	-2.85	12/31/71	+6.11	+23.62
12/31/03	+25.32	+33.81	12/31/70	+4.82	+6.96
12/31/02	-16.76	+3.13	12/31/69	-15.19	-15.34
12/31/01	-7.10	+2.06	12/31/68	+4.27	+2.08
12/31/00	-6.17	-11.10	12/31/67	+15.20	+3.04
12/31/99	+25.22	+15.80	12/31/66	-18.94	-12.85
12/31/98	+16.10	-1.22	12/31/65	+10.88	+4.93
12/31/97	+22.64	+1.17	12/31/64	+14.57	+5.95
12/31/96	+26.01	+18.78	12/31/63	+17.00	+7.42
12/31/95	+33.45	+26.25	12/31/62	-10.81	-16.63
12/31/94	+2.14	-1.02	12/31/61	+18.71	+12.28
12/31/93	+13.72	+6.20	12/31/60	-9.34	-12.65
12/31/92	+4.17	+2.35	12/31/59	+16.40	+20.93
12/31/91	+20.32	+7.35	12/31/58	+33.96	+19.55
12/31/90	-4.34	-8.06	12/31/57	-12.77	-11.71
12/31/89	+26.96	+16.86	12/31/56	+2.27	-1.11
12/31/88	+11.85	+11.21	12/31/55	+20.77	+10.01
12/31/87	+2.26	+17.71	12/31/54	+43.96	+26.83

Date	DOW Yearly Percent Return	DOW Yearly % Return without including the days that Mars was within 30 degrees of the lunar node
12/31/53	-3.77	+0.30
12/31/52	+8.42	+0.61
12/31/51	+14.36	+15.16
12/31/50	+17.41	+15.35
12/31/49	+13.10	+13.78
12/31/48	-2.13	-6.41
12/31/47	+2.24	-4.30
12/31/46	-8.14	-19.01
12/31/45	+26.97	+2.21
12/31/44	+11.80	+2.79
12/31/43	+13.81	+7.50
12/31/42	+7.61	+3.05
12/31/41	-15.38	-16.89
12/31/40	-12.57	-6.51
12/31/39	-2.83	+4.91
12/31/38	+27.73	+36.04
12/31/37	-32.82	-4.69
12/31/36	+24.82	+16.96
12/31/35	+38.53	+28.24
12/31/34	+5.44	-2.65
12/31/33	+63.74	+17.17
12/31/32	-22.64	+36.22
12/31/31	-52.67	-29.61
12/31/30	-33.77	-16.34
12/31/29	-17.17	+22.13
12/31/28	+49.48	+30.55
12/31/27	+27.67	+14.35
12/31/26	+0.35	+14.93
12/31/25	+30.00	+17.46
12/31/24	+26.16	+8.36
12/31/23	-2.70	-7.30
12/31/22	+21.50	+18.15
12/31/21	+6.13	-7.45
12/31/20	-37.63	-33.61
12/31/19	+28.00	+9.31
12/31/18	+11.63	+11.31
12/31/17	-21.94	-5.29
12/31/16	-2.56	+13.49
12/31/15	+61.89	+31.81
12/31/14	-32.65	-20.64
12/31/13	-10.04	-0.59
12/31/12	+7.78	+7.34
12/31/11	+1.07	+8.59
12/31/10	-18.21	-7.38
12/31/09	+14.60	+17.95
12/31/08	+39.95	+27.95
12/31/07	-44.45	-13.27
12/31/06	-0.95	-16.01
12/31/05	+33.55	+17.78
12/31/04	+36.29	+18.58
12/31/03	-24.69	-9.06
12/31/02	+0.49	-1.74
12/31/01	-6.88	+0.14
12/31/00	+8.48	+20.50
12/31/99	+11.34	+7.30
12/31/98	+22.50	+28.46
12/31/97	+21.57	+7.53

In 2020, the Dow Jones rose +7.25%.

Earlier in 2020, it dropped -27.25% during the time when Mars was within 30 degrees of the lunar node between January 15th and April 3rd. The rest of the year when Mars was not within that 30 degrees of the lunar node, the Dow Jones was up +46.79%.

Here are future dates of when Mars will be within 30 degrees of the lunar node.

November 1, 2021 - January 23, 2022
June 23, 2022 - September 17, 2022
January 13, 2023 - January 24, 2023
August 21, 2023 - November 16, 2023
April 11, 2024 - June 24, 2024
June 4, 2025 - September 4, 2025
February 3, 2026 - April 18, 2026
September 26, 2026 - January 10, 2027
April 2, 2027 - June 11, 2027

In 2020, Mars was within 30 degrees of the lunar node from January 15 and remained there until April 3rd. Below is a diagram of how Mars within that 30 degree orb applies on an astrology chart:

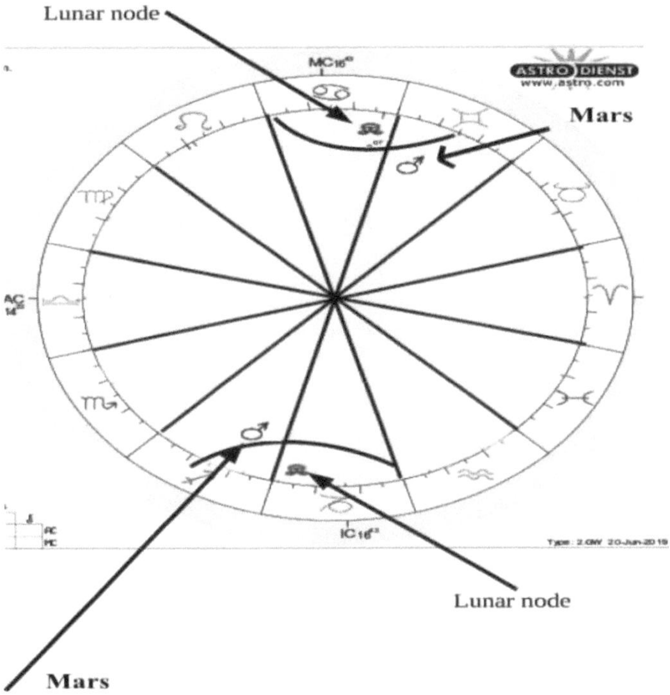

In the data of the Dow Jones going back to 1896, the Mars retrograde phases in which the planet Mars was going backwards within 30 degrees of the lunar node was not factored into the data as being within 30 degrees of the lunar node.

So we see in 2020, the Dow Jones dropped 27% between January 15 and April 3rd when Mars was within 30 degrees of the lunar node. On January 30th, the World Health Organization declared the COVID-19 outbreak to be an international public health crisis. The implications for the global supply chain was a catalyst for the stock market sell-off. The most severe drops occurred on March 9th, 12th, and 16th, when the Dow Jones fell -7.81%, -9.99%, and -12.93% respectively. US Treasury yields also plunged during this time, which indicates a higher demand for Treasury securities. Treasury securities are usually much safer for investors and a higher demand usually indicates pessimism towards the higher risk securities like stocks. From February 17th - 21st, "10-year and 30-year U.S. Treasury securities fell to 1.56% and 2.00% respectively" Yields continued to fall until around March 10th.

In April , the Dow Jones began to recover when Mars was no longer within 30 degrees of the lunar node. The key element in presenting this is the attempt to foster the idea of applying seasonal interest rates, or a fixed

interest rate setting policy that would automatically set interest rates based around Mars being within 30 degrees of the lunar node. The point of the Federal Reserve is to set monetary policy and also deter bank runs by setting rates according to economic projections, mitigating the dangers arising from black swan events, or unforeseen drastic declines in the market. It has come to the attention that the Federal Reserve, in bringing elasticity to fiscal policy has garnered them a significant level of clout, perhaps an excessive amount according to some of the pundits. The Mars hypothesis provides a solution or an answer that would cool those sentiments. By putting the history into context, the Federal Reserve implementing a fixed interest rate setting policy would give those seeking non-human intervention a sense of relief. Setting interest rates would now take on a constitutional framework. Many economists maintain a premise that improper use of interest rate policy is one of the factors that led to the 2007 -2008 stock market crash. The Federal Reserve's continued cuts of interest rates after the 9/ 11 terror attacks--even as the market remained sluggish amidst those cuts--led to the housing boom and bust.

The Mars hypothesis does not have to warrant some type of cosmic sensationalism that would repel any sound fundamental due-diligence. However, since Mars is hypothesized to effect situations negatively, one can use such a thesis to project when negative events which are fundamentally tied to economics would take place. One can simply observe when Mars is within 30 degrees of the lunar node and anticipate for some negative event to arise and challenge investor confidence. In the book "Ares Le Mandat", there is presented a number of events which take place during this Mars/Lunar node alignment, events which can easily be relegated to having economic implications. There is a historical backdrop that can be applied to a fundamental study of stock market projections.

This constitutional element brought forth by the Mars hypothesis would also put to rest much of the grievances put out by theories related to market manipulation. There is a certain degree of impatience that comes with a longer term market upswing phase, where investor anticipation and a subsequent non-manifestation of a downswing(within a reasonable time-frame) brings about accusations and theories concerning unfair human intervention on the stock market. The purpose of this writing is to not only hypothesize that the Federal Reserve can set interest rates based on the position of the planet Mars, but also demonstrate exactly how and at the same time, formulate a system that would enable the Federal Reserve to carry out its application in real time.

The framework laid out in this writing will center around 2 astrological parameters that will attempt to account for bear market phases and the low point during that time. In recent years, the market has retested bear market lows during anticipated bull market phases that immediately followed. Most notably were the ones that took place in 2009 and 2003. After the bear market/recession phase of late 2008, the actual market low did not occur until March of 2009. The same happened in late 2002/early 2003 where the low did not occur until March 2003, retesting the lower levels which occurred during the bear market phase of 2002. This issue of projecting the market low of a recession or correction phase is key to optimizing interest rate decision making. The first parameter has already been explained; it's Mars's transit within 30 degrees of the lunar node on either side of the lunar node(not counting when Mars goes retrograde during that transit). The second parameter is the Sun's transit within 30 degrees of the lunar node, but only the transit in which the Sun is situated opposite of the lunar node.

1st Parameter 2nd Parameter

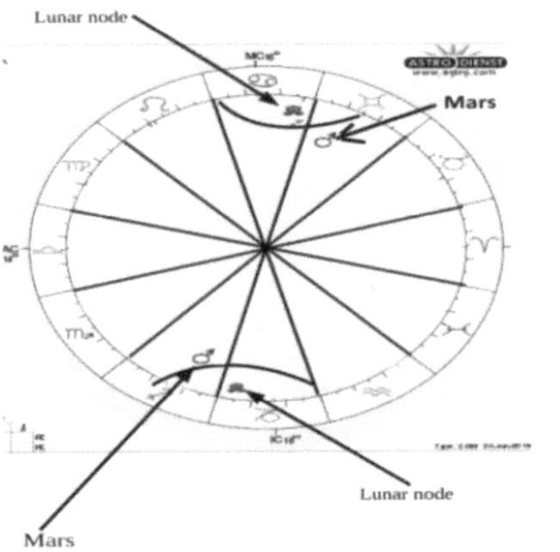

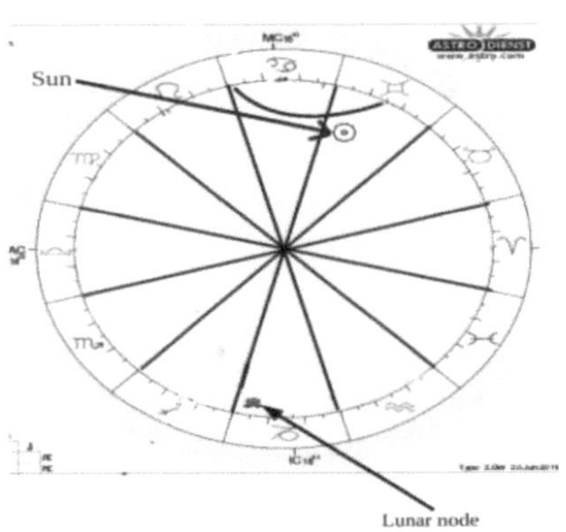

In the 1st Parameter above, Mars is at a 30 degree orb--both conjunct and opposite--to the lunar node position. This falls under how we define "Mars within 30 degrees of the lunar node" The 2nd Parameter shown above is defined under "Sun being within 30 degrees of the lunar node, but opposite to the actual position of the lunar node." This transit of the Sun will be used to project the start of a year's bear market phase. The ensuing transit of Mars going within 30 degrees of the lunar node as indicated in the 1st parameter will project when the low point of that bear market phase should occur. A system revolving around these parameters will hypothesize for interest rates to be increased when the Sun enters within 30 degrees of the lunar node(as shown in the 2nd parameter), and to be decreased following the time frame of the ensuing transit of Mars within 30 degrees of the lunar node as shown in the 1st parameter. During this ensuing transit of Mars, one can hypothesize that the low of the recession or correction phase will occur, making it the ideal time for initiating interest rate cuts and other forms of quantitative easing. Applying this system back in 2020 will allow us to start the recession phase projection when the sun entered within 30 degrees of the lunar node in December of 2019. See example on the next page.

In the chart below, the sun entered within 30 degrees of the lunar node on December 1st 2019. We see the trajectory of its transit within the 30 degree orb of the lunar node position displayed opposite the sun. This is where policy would project a bear market phase and raise interest rates as a result.

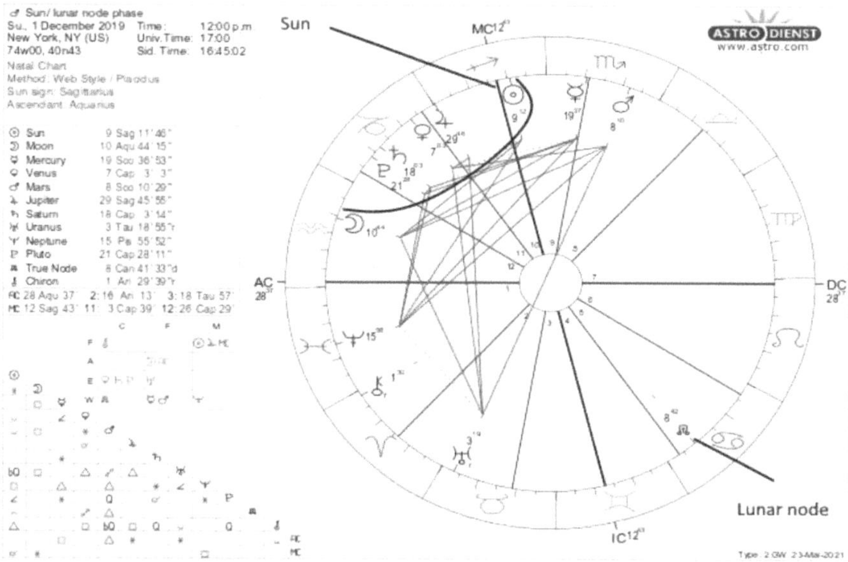

Below is the ensuing transit of Mars within 30 degrees of the lunar node starting on January 15th 2020 and lasting until April 3rd, 2020. The trajectory of this transit is shown in the chart below.

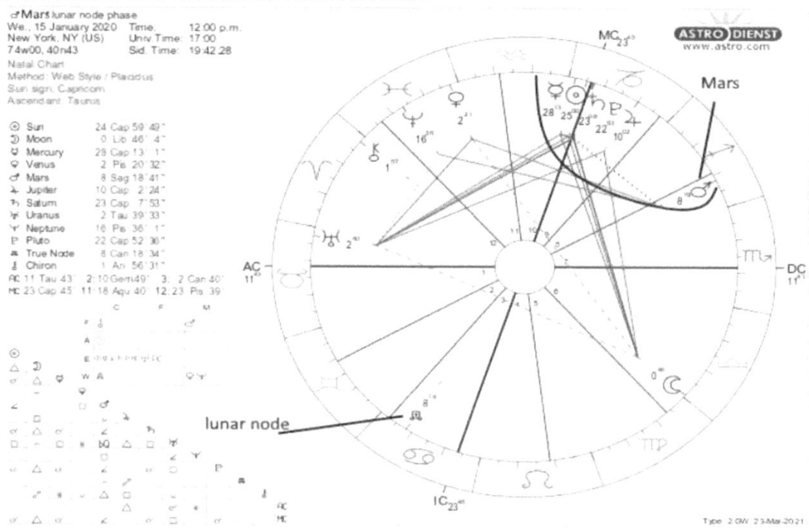

Ideally, the Federal Reserve would began the process of initiating interest rate cuts after this Mars/Lunar node phase would end. The market hit its lows in March of 2020. After this, the market recovered considerably throughout 2020.

This system would allow the Federal Reserve to maintain a greater control over inflation, in so much that the Mars/lunar node phase would aid in projecting accurately both black swan events and market bottoms. Setting interest rates lower during a recession phase long before the market reaches its lows puts the monetary system at risk of inflation when the market does not respond to those interest rate cuts, leaving policy makers having to continually cut rates. When interest rates are lowered, consumers tend to borrow more and also spend more. As the money supply becomes inflated, the purchasing power of money begins to erode as the price of goods began to rise. This is what happened back starting in 2000, and it led to the housing crisis in 2007 when borrowing and debt leveraging went out of control. This system of using the Sun, Mars, and the lunar node will provide a strategy to anticipate market bottoms, allowing policy makers to then embark appropriately on provisions to begin cutting interest rates.

The Mars strategy does not entail that one would detect the exact day of the market bottom. It does however, aid a policy outlook that would mark the end of the Mars/lunar node phase as the ideal time to presume that the low of that bear market phase has already taken place. This should also deter deflationary prospects that would arise upon retest should such be incorrectly considered a longer term bearish indicator. If one presumes that the market would not respond to interest rate cuts, then it's plausible that in attempting to avoid an inflationary scenario, policy can deem themselves justified to leave rates unchanged or raise them over time. A very unfavorable scenario if the market rises amidst increasingly higher rates, making it more difficult to raise interest rates at the appropriate time .

With this system, we can presumably change how the fiscal year is applied to the Federal Reserve. In shifting to a fixed interest rate setting policy, we automatically fall into a floating fiscal year, in which the beginning of that year would start when the Sun enters within 30 degrees of the lunar node (opposite the position of the lunar node). At this, a bear market is automatically projected to take place at the start of every fiscal year, with the ensuing transit of Mars within 30 degrees of the lunar node serving as our time frame for that year's market low. In this application, we are using interest rate in an active sense in order to exert some control over the market. Typically, the Federal Reserve raises interest rates to cool down an overbought market. When the recession follows, the FED then lowers rates near the end of the recession to stimulate buying. Here, we apply interest rates in a way that affirms projections and exerts some control over the market ups and downs.

In 2019, the Dow Jones set 22 record highs. The market rose continuously throughout the entire year. The low for the year took place at the beginning of the year, since that bearish phase had its origins from late 2018. Using our our new system, we can apply our projection for 2019, by observing the Sun's transit of the lunar node position, which took place in late 2018, starting December 19, 2018.

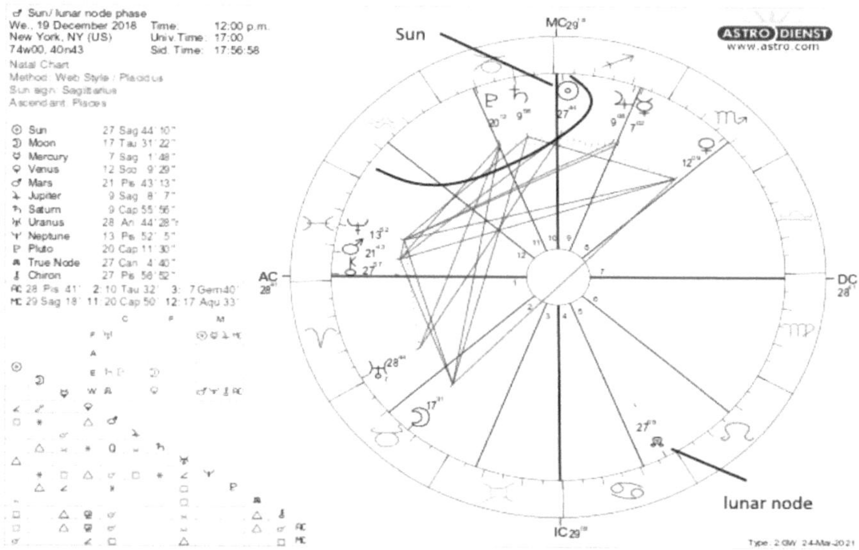

Theoretically, we can follow protocol and project a bear market phase to begin here and wait for Mars to enter within 30 degrees of the lunar node, so that we can anticipate the low point of this phase. Here is the Dow Jones chart for 2018 and 2019

The ensuing Mars/lunar node phase took place between April 30, 2019 - July 28, 2019. The ending of this phase ensured that the market correction projected from December 19, 2018 was over.

After July 28th 2019, the Federal Reserve could have begun rate cuts to stimulate the economy, at least until December 1st of later that year when the Sun would re-enter within 30 degrees of the lunar node, setting off a bearish indicator.

In going back to early 2018, we notice that the Dow Jones peaked in late January and entered market correction on February 8th. Our system accounts for this since the Sun entered within 30 degrees of the lunar node on January 5th, 2018. This where we would theoretically have anticipated a correction phase.

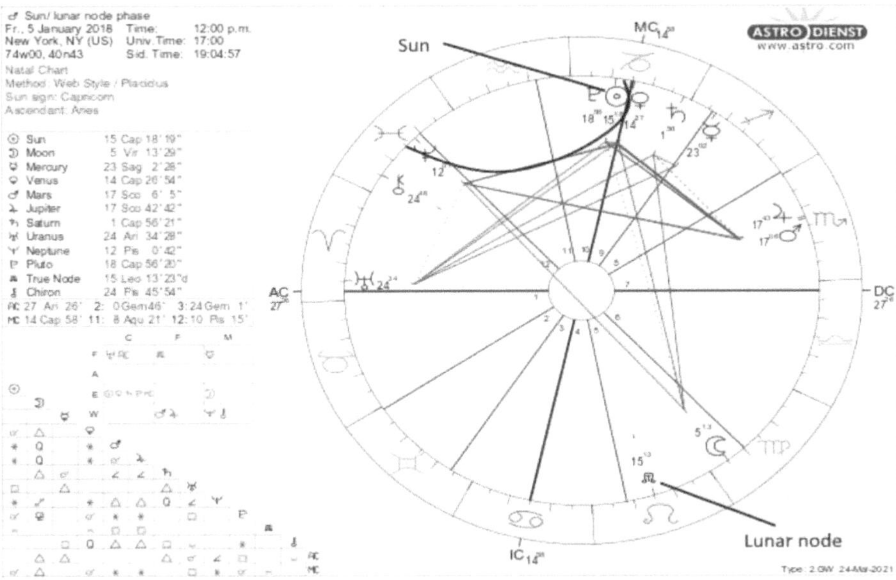

From there, we would wait until Mars would enter and complete its transit within 30 degrees of the lunar node before decreasing interest rates. The ensuing Mars transit 30 degrees of the lunar node took place from April 8th 2018 until June 26th 2018. We had to cut the transit short initially because Mars went retrograde during the transit on June 27th. When this happens, we no longer count Mars as being within 30 degrees of the lunar node for the duration of the retrograde phase. The retrograde phase ended on August 27. Mars was within 30 degrees of the lunar node when it ended, and because of that we resume counting Mars as being within 30 degrees of the lunar node. So from August 28th, 2018 - November 14th 2018 when the Mars/ lunar node phase officially ended, we still anticipate that market lows from the earlier projected correction phase has already taken place.

This would give us a small window of opportunity to cut interest rates before our next bearish indicator which would have taken place on December 19, 2018, when the sun en-tered within 30 degrees of the lunar node. We could have also cut rates during the Mars retrograde phase. Here is the Dow Jones chart for 2018.

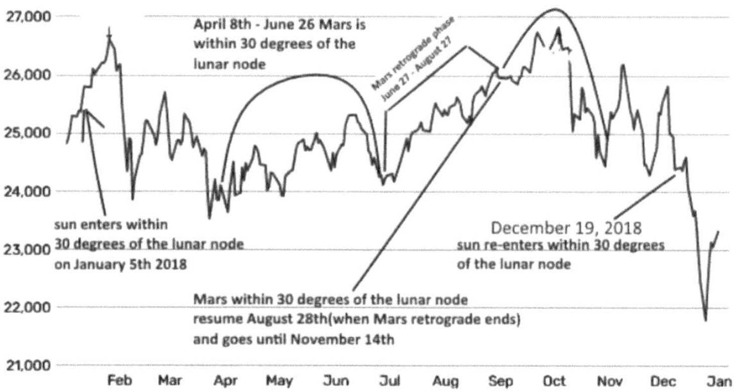

This gives us a good overview, where the Federal Reserve could have raised interest rates starting on January 5th, looked for the bottom to have taken place when Mars was with 30 degrees of the lunar node from April 8th - June 26, then begin cutting rates when the Mars retrograde phase started, raise rates again when the Mars retrograde ended August 27th, looked for the bottom again as Mars within 30 degrees of the lunar node resumed August 28th thru November 14th, cut rates again following the end of the Mars/lunar node phase on November 14, and then finally raise rates on December 19th 2018 when the sun entered within 30 degrees of the lunar node, indicating a bearish phase.

In 2017, numerous records were set by the Dow Jones Industrial average. 3 times that year, the Dow Jones had 9 days of consecutive gains. The Dow Jones also rose 8th months in a row during the year. There was also 5 1000 point milestones achieved by the index. On Jan. 25, 2017, the index closed at 20,068.51.2. On March 1, 2017, it closed above 21,000. On Aug. 2, 2017, it reached 22,000. On October 18th, it closed at 23000. A month later, it went to 24000. If we apply our system to 2017, we see that our bearish indicator which is the sun within 30 degrees of the lunar node took place starting January 23, 2017

We see in the chart below that the Sun began its transit within 30 degrees of the lunar node, setting off a bearish indicator. However, Mars is already situated within 30 degrees of the lunar node and will finish that transit shortly on Feb 1st 2017.

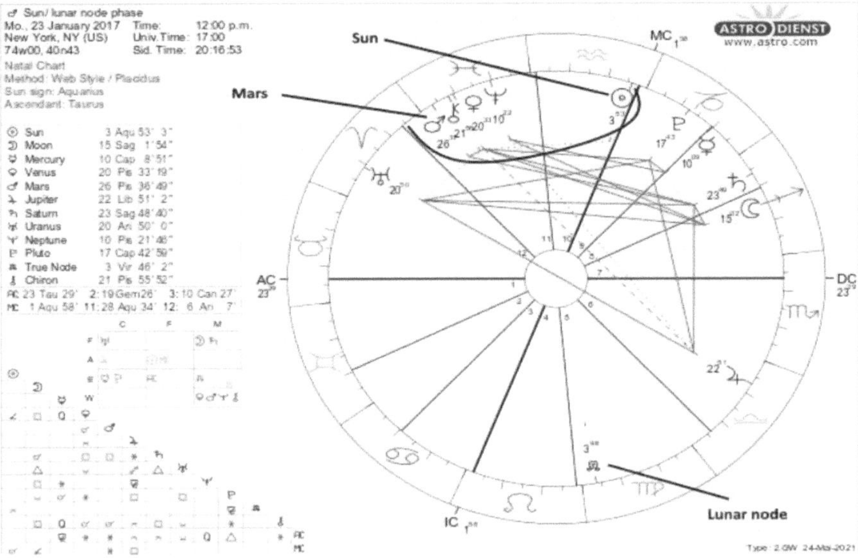

This information will allow us to presume that the ensuing Mars/lunar node phase is already in motion at the start of this bearish indicator set off by the Sun/lunar node phase. We can also posit that the low of this bearish phase will have already occurred come Feb 1st when the Mars/lunar node phase ends. Here is the Dow Jones chart for 2017

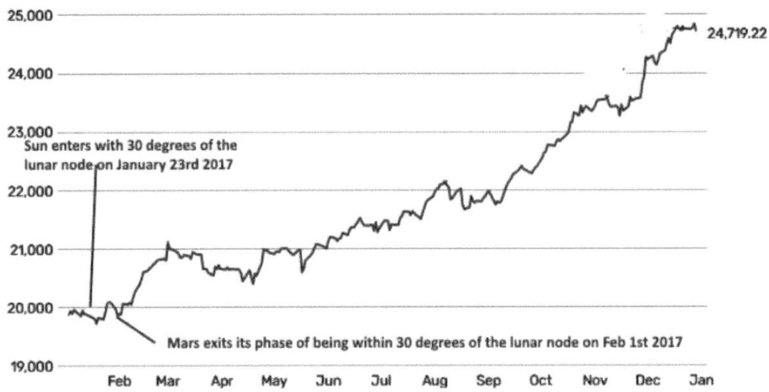

The low for the year occurred on January 20th, 2017 when the Dow went to 19,732.. just before our declaration of a bear market on January 23 when the Sun entered within 30 degrees of the lunar node. The Dow retested at 19,864 on January 31st, 2017, a few days after going above 20,000. With the ensuing Mars already within 30 degrees of the lunar node, hypothetically the Federal Reserve would have been able to conclude--after the Mars/ lunar node phased finished--that the low for that bear market phase has been reached. Henceforth, they could begin a series of rate cuts until the next Sun/lunar node phase in 2018.

In 2016, The Dow Jones began the year very sluggish. On January 4th, the Dow dropped 160 points. In 3 days, it fell another 5%. In late January, investors began to panic over plummeting oil prices. On February 11, the Dow reached its low for the year at 15, 660. There was a brief crash in June when the market dropped 600+ points on June 24th after news of Britain's declaration to depart from the European Union (BREXIT). In the late summer months of July and August, however, the Dow Jones rose as European investors began to invest in US equities, fearing Brexit implications. The market then rose considerably in November when Donald Trump became United States President Elect, giving investors renewed confidence in the market.

If we apply the astrological factors, we see that the Sun entered with 30 degrees of the Lunar node on February 11th, the day the Dow Jones reached its low for the year. .

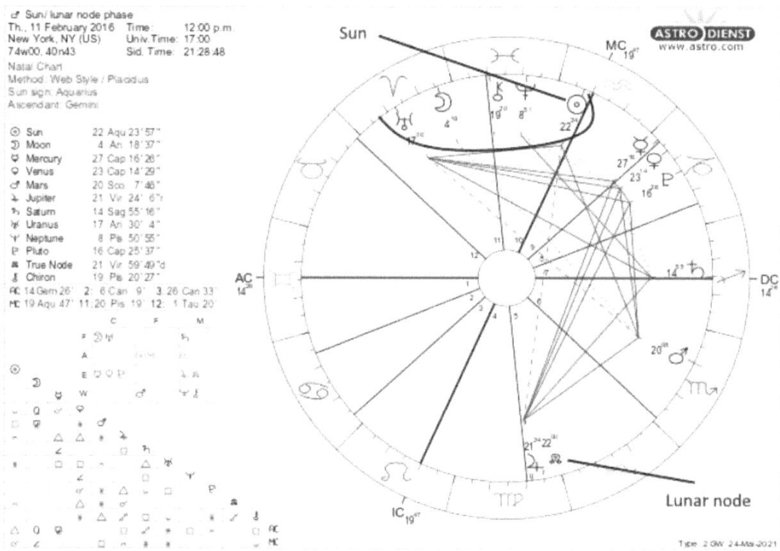

The ensuing Mars phase within 30 degrees of the lunar node began did not began until November 21 and didn't end until Feb 1st 2017. Hypothetically, the Federal Reserve applying this astrological outlook would have been raising interest rates throughout the entire year of 2016.

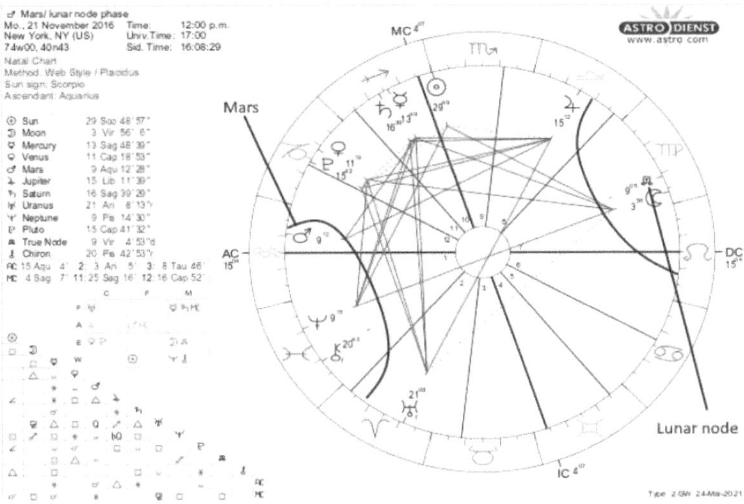

In 2015, the Dow Jones began the year on a positive note. The high for the year occurred in May. Later in August, however, the Dow Jones dropped significantly. It dropped 531 points on August 21, and on August 24, Black Monday, it fell 1,089 points right after the open. China's Yuan devaluation brought forth a sense of pessimism amongst investors regarding how the FED(Federal Reserve) would apply interest rates.

Astrologically speaking, our bearish indicator which is Sun going within 30 degrees of the lunar node took place on March 1st 2015

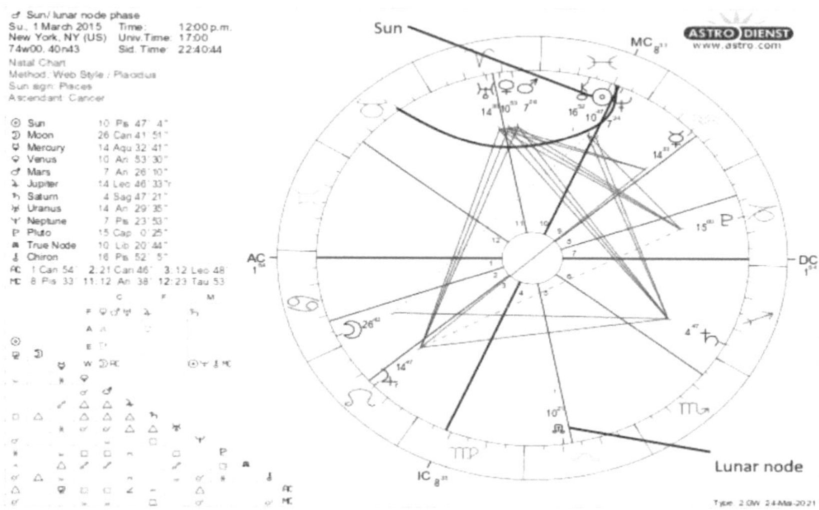

Theoretically, projection of a bear market is declared here. The ensuing Mars phase is already within 30 degrees of the lunar node. It completes its phase on April 13, 2015. From there Federal Reserve could begin cutting interest rates until the Sun goes within 30 degrees of the lunar node again February 11, 2016. For 2015, this turns out to be disastrous since the market dipped significantly in August, theoretically during a time where this astrological system would have been calling for interest rate cuts. The crash occurred on August 24th. Coincidentally the Sun did enter within 30 degrees of the lunar node, but on the same side of the position of the lunar node. We established for this algorithm that only the Sun within 30 degrees of the lunar node--but opposite the position of the lunar node-- would be applied to what we consider our bearish indicator. Based on what we have established so far, application of this system would have failed significantly in 2015. The only option to keep this system going would be to blame Judaism's Shmita year as the reason for the break or malfunction. The Shmita year for 2015 took place between September 14, 2014 and September 14, 2015. A simple workaround would be for the Federal Reserve to apply diligence to this occurrence and simply change the Sun/ lunar node indicator to when the Sun is within 30 degrees of the lunar node on the same side or conjunct the position of the lunar node.

The Shmita year is part of the Jewish Cycle of time in which just as there is a sabbath day of rest within a 7 day cycle, there is also a sabbatical year of rest within a 7 year cycle. Throughout this writing, I will continue to apply the astrological system as established at the beginning of this thesis, but will note the time when the Shmita year is in effect, so that the reader can take that into account when the astrological system doesn't qualify appropriately during a Shmita year.

In 2014, the Dow Jones reached its low in February that year before climbing steadily until it went into a correction phase from late July until mid-October. Late October, the Federal Reserve announced that they would not raise interest rates until 2015. The market responded to close out the year on a positive not.

***Alert: Keep in mind the Judiasm Shmita year goes from September 14, 2014 and September 14, 2015, which may compromise our application of the astrological parameters.**

In applying the astrological system to 2014, we see the Sun entered within 30 degrees of the lunar node on March 19th 2014

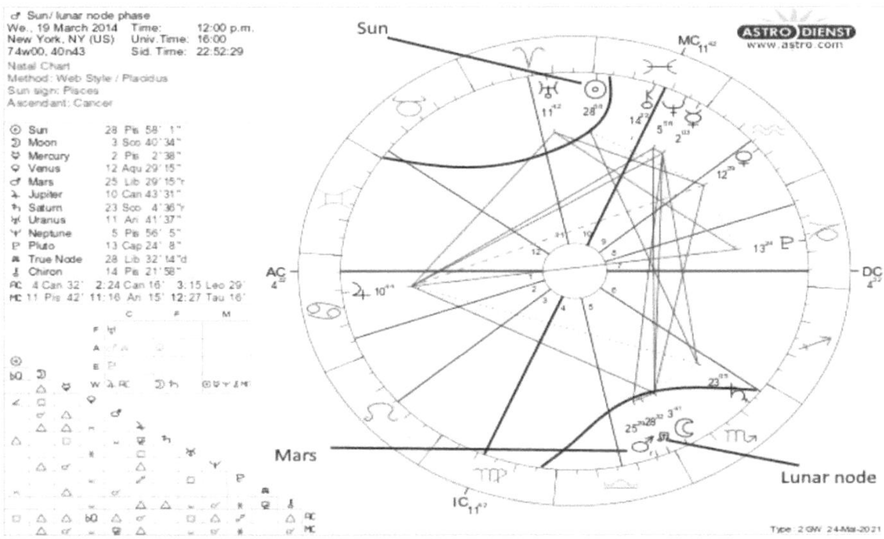

The ensuing Mars transit within 30 degrees of the lunar node is in retrograde. (Keep in mind that Mars is within 30 degrees of the lunar node on both the conjunct and opposite side of the position of the lunar node in this thesis.) Theoretically the Federal Reserve would begin raising rate at this bearish indicator. The ensuing Mars does not count as being within 30 degrees of the lunar node until the retrograde phase end on May 18. So from May 19th - August 29th, Mars goes within 30 degrees of the lunar node. The bottom should have occurred before that transit ended. After, August 29th, the Federal reserve can start the process of cutting interest rates. Before, rates would have been raised from the time the Sun entered within 30 degrees of the lunar node on March 19th until the time Mars finished its transit within 30 degrees of the lunar node on August 29th. The bottom for the year happened in February before our Sun indicator, but retested somewhat in August when Mars was within 30 degrees of the lunar node. On September 14th , the Shmita year began and would have discombobulated our astrological projections during that Shmita year timeframe.

In 2013, the Dow Jones rose 26%. It rose above 15,000 in May. Near the end of the year, the Federal Reserve's decided to scale back the size of its monthly bond purchases, which didn't deter investor optimism as the market rallied in response. Earlier in the year, speculation around whether or not the Federal Reserve would scale back its Quantitative Easing program rattled the markets.

On April 6th 2013, our bearish indicator, the Sun entered within 30 degrees of the lunar node, marking the time when the Federal Reserve would theoretically start raising rates. The ensuing Mars phase within 30 degrees of the lunar node is already in motion.

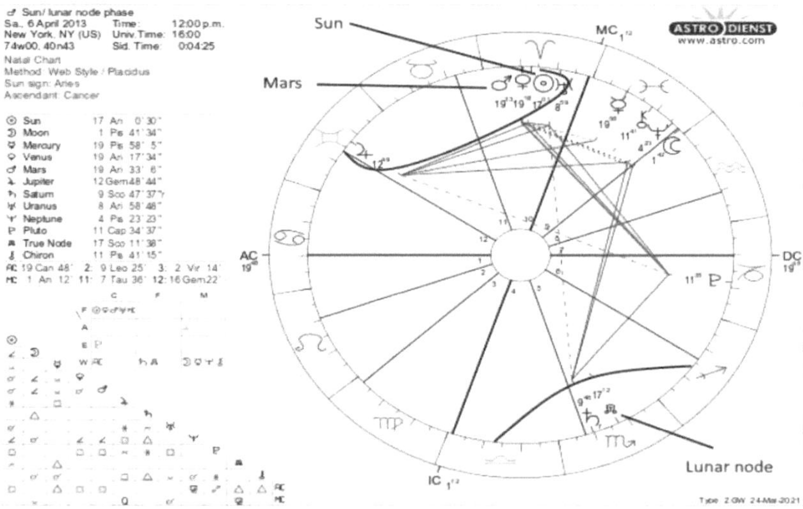

It exits that transit on June 23rd, 2013. From there, the low for that phase would be deemed to have already taken place. The Federal Reserve theoretically would then begin cutting rates and stimulating the market. From June 24th, the market climbed steadily thru the remainder of the year. Here is the chart for 2013. The Federal Reserve would have begun raising rates on April 6, 2013 and began cutting them from June 24th 2013

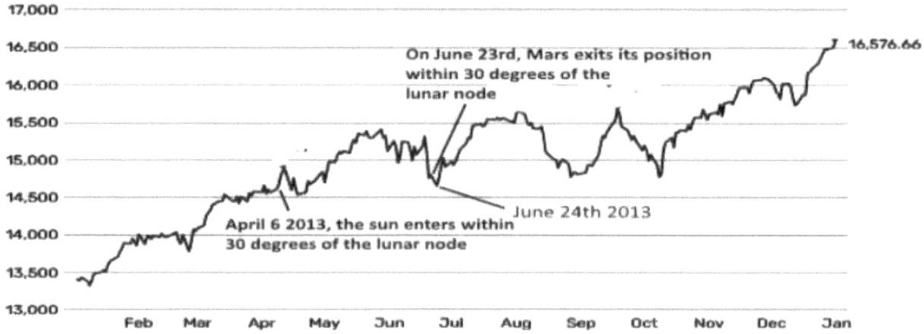

In 2012, the Dow Jones achieved its 4th consecutive year of gains, finishing the year up 7%. The Federal Reserve continued to apply its lose monetary policies as the market was still recovering from the 2008 financial crisis. The Senate also averted a massive fiscal cliff of government spending cuts and increased taxes intended for 2013.

On April 25, 2012, the Sun entered within 30 degrees of the lunar node, which is when we project a bear market to occur.

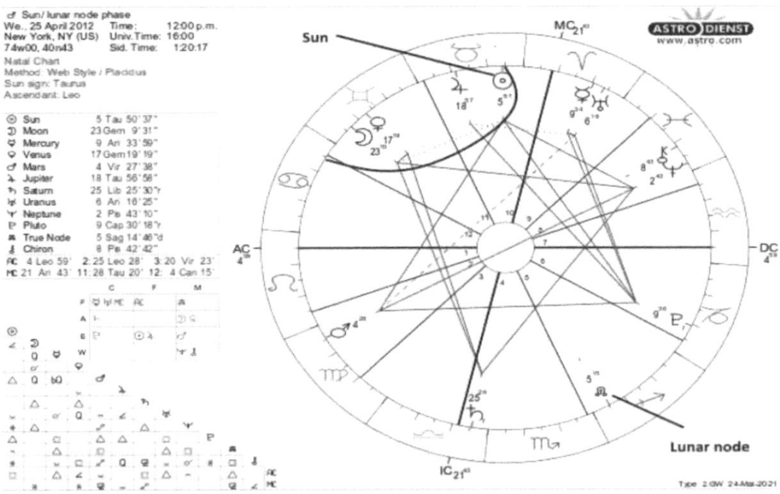

The ensuing Mars/lunar node phase began on Aug 23, 2012 and ended on November 12 2012. In applying this astrological methodology in real time, the Federal Reserve would have begun raising interest rate from April 25th when the Sun entered its position within 30 degrees of the lunar node. The FED would started slashing rates from November 12th 2012, when the ensuing Mars/lunar node phase ended.

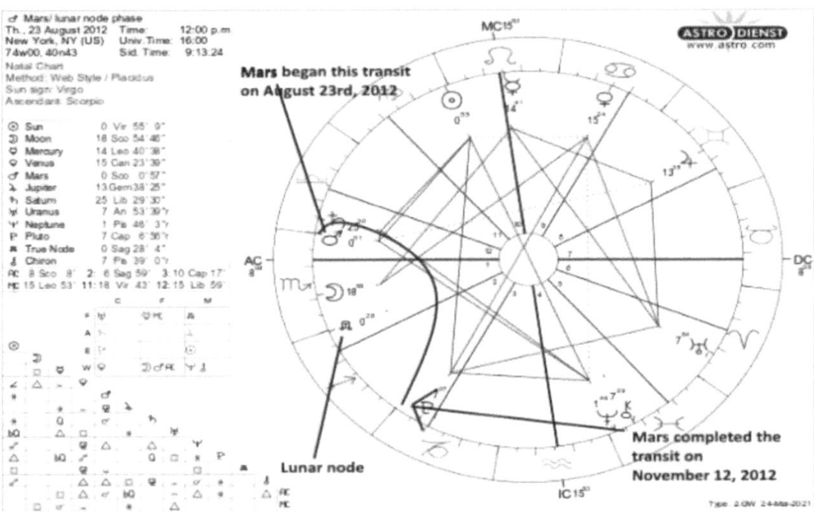

Here is the chart for the Dow Jones in 2012 and where the astrological parameters would fit:

We see that projecting a bear market with our Sun indicator would have applied accordingly in 2012. The ensuing Mars phase shows some attempt to retest the previous low just when Mars is getting ready to complete the transit. It would have been feasible to raise interest rates from April 25 2012 to November 12th 2012 before applying cuts through the remainder of the year.

In 2011, the Dow Jones began the year rising 4% by early March before being rattled briefly by the earthquake and tsunami that struck Japan on March 11th. Afterwards, The Dow recovered slightly for a few months until late July when the August 2nd deadline for a spending bill approached. The delay caused concern for investors, and when the credit-rating agency Standard & Poor's announced that it had downgraded the U.S. from AAA to AA a few days later, the market began to decline further throughout August. The Dow resumed a volatile upswing late in the year, finishing the year 2011 up 5.5%.

The application of the astrological system would have initiated on May 14th 2011 when the Sun entered within 30 degrees of the lunar node.

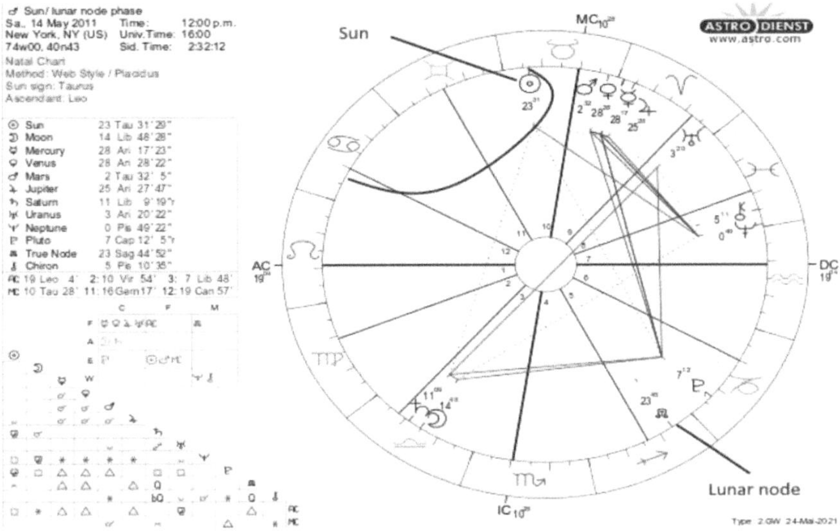

From that point, the Federal Reserve would theoretically begin the course of raising interest rates and wait for the ensuing Mars/lunar node phase to complete. The ensuing Mars/lunar node phase began on June 11, 2011 and lasted until September 1st 2011.

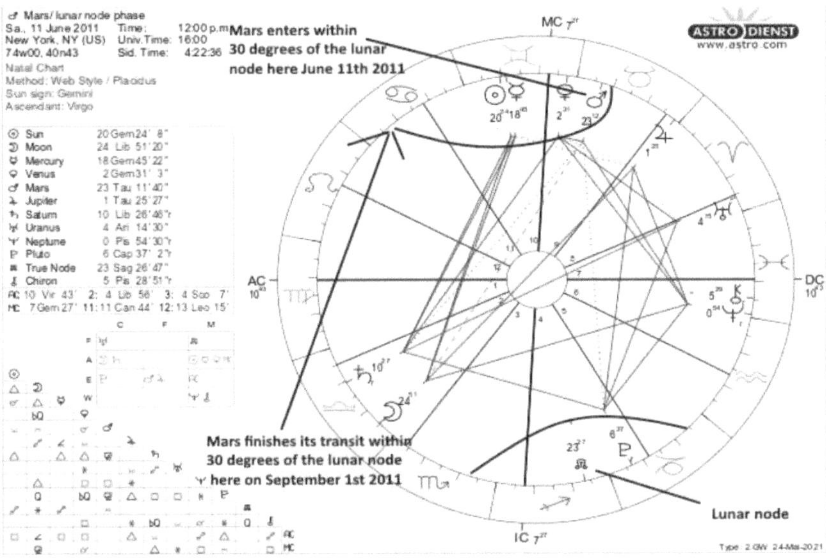

These astrological parameters applied to the year 2011 provide us with a protocol in which the Federal Reserve would begin raising interest rates from May 14th 2011 until September 1st 2011, projecting a correction to take place during that time. After which, the FED would begin cutting interest rates for the remainder of the year. Here is the chart for the Dow Jones in 2011 and how the astrological parameters would have applied that year

Once again the projections based on astrological factors would have applied favorably to market conditions.

In 2010, the Dow Jones rose 11%. Half of that occurred in the final month of December that year. The major component of 2010 occurred in May when the market crashed on May 6th. However, A 600 Billion dollar stimulus plan from the Federal Reserve helped the market recover from its May-June worries over the "Flash Crash" that took place on May 6th when the market dropped 900 points within minutes before recovering a large portion of those losses. The causes of the flash crash have been speculated to revolve around the use of high frequency trading algorithms along with technical glitches in the reporting of prices on the NYSE(New York Stock Exchange).

The Sun entered with 30 degrees of the lunar node on June 2nd 2010, after the Flash Crash on May 6th. Hypothetically the Federal Reserve would have announced bearish projections. The ensuing Mars phase does not begin its transit until November 2nd 2010. It completes the phase on January 18, 2011. This sets our time-frame of theoretical interest rate increases from June 2, 2010 - January 18, 2011.

Here is the astrological chart where the Sun sets off a bearish indicator on June 2nd 2010.

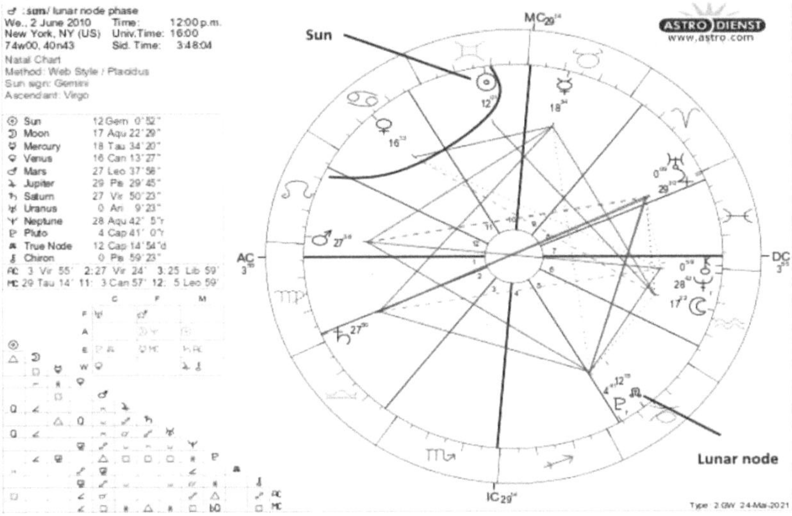

Here is the Mars transit within 30 degrees of the lunar node.

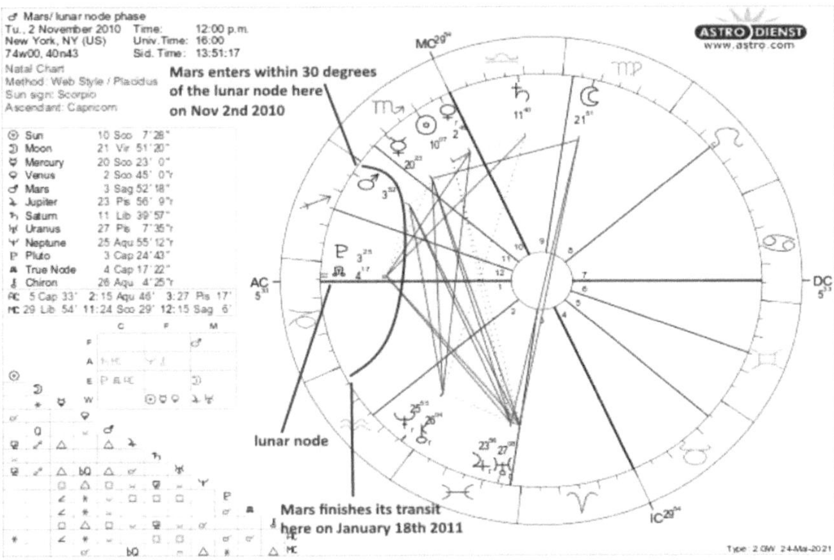

Here is the Dow Jones chart for the year 2010 with the astrological parameter dates included:

The market didn't dip too far during this astrologically projected correction phase. It actually rose steadily beginning in September of 2010. However, after January 18th 2011 the market did climb until the next bearish indicator which occurred in May of 2011 when the Sun went within 30 degrees of the lunar node.

For the year 2009, the Dow Jones finished the year up 19%. A number of companies beat out analyst expectation. Optimism about market recovery from the 2008 crash also propelled stocks forward, and a weak dollar raised investor hopes concerning US exports.

In 2009, our bearish indicator occurred on June 21 2009 when the sun entered within 30 degrees of the lunar node. The ensuing Mars transit within 30 degrees of the lunar node began August 24th 2009 was cut short on December 20 2009 when Mars went retrograde. It didn't resume its transit until March 11th when Mars retrograde ended and finally completed the transit on May 4th, just 2 days before the "Flash Crash"

Here is the Dow Jones chart for the year 2009 with the astrological parameter dates included:

We can see that our astrological based projections do not match up exactly with the what happened in 2009. From June 21st 2009 to December 20, 2009 which is when we would have anticipated a bear market, the chart shows that the Dow did not drop at all during that time. Theoretically, we would have been raising interest rates throughout that time-frame.

In 2008, the Dow Jones experienced one of its worst years, dropping 33%. The Housing bubble and debt bubble were considered major triggers for the 2008 crash. During the housing bubble, investment firms were packaging mortgage loans into insecurities(Mortgage-backed securities-MBS), and then selling them off to investors, allowing the firm to keep them off their financial statements. Rating agencies rated the MBS, which served as a benchmark for potential buyers. The investors then started using credit default swaps, in which an insurance company would guarantee to cover the any potential losses from the MBS in exchange for a premium. This proved profitable for many investors and insurance companies. However, when investment firms started having trouble finding buyers for their MBS products, along with rating agencies downgrading them as the credit crisis worsened, investment firms were left having to hold large positions in MBS. This is what happened to Bear Sterns in April of 2008 and then Lehman brothers in September of 2008, as both had to declare bankruptcy. AIG, the main underwriter of credit default swaps was bailed out by the Federal Reserve. since the company was designate as Too Big To Fail. AIG provided protections worth half a trillion dollars, 300 billion to banks in the US and Europe. Failure of AIG would have had global implications.

Before presenting the application of the astrological system to 2008, I want add that a Judaism Shmita year took place from September, 30 2007 - September 30, 2008. Keep in mind that this could discombobulate our projections, showing them to be way off from what actually happened.

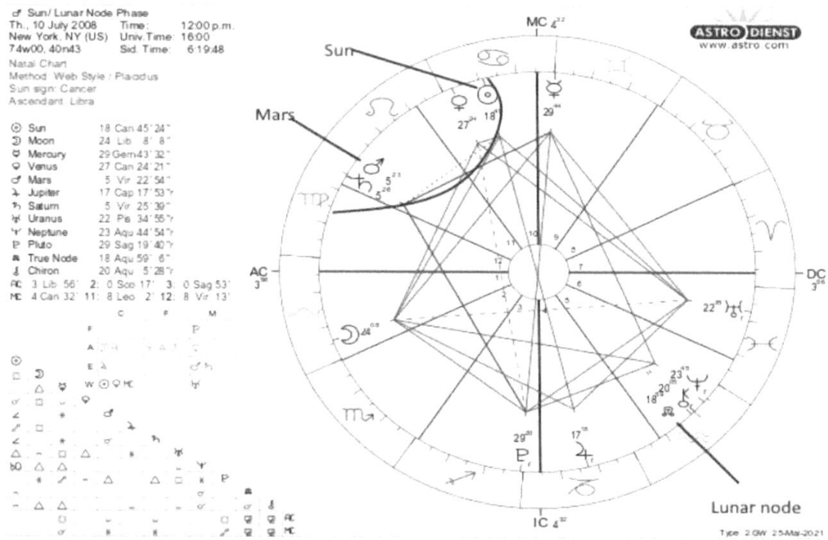

We see that, hypothetically we would set a projection of bear market to begin here on July 10, 2008. The ensuing Mars phase is already in motion and completes its transit on August 1st 2008. According to our thesis the low for the year would have occurred between July 10 and August 1.

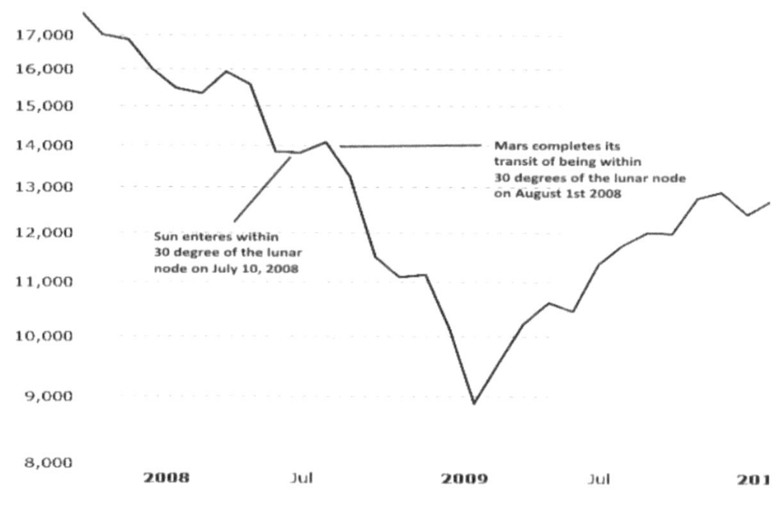

We can see that applying our astrological parameters in 2008 sets our projections way off since we would have anticipated a bullish market after Mars completed its transit of being within 30 degrees of the lunar node. The Judaism Shmita year has to be blamed for this fallibility. Perhaps delaying when we apply our ensuing Mars transit during a Shmita year could serve as a workaround. in 2008, if we would have postponed out ensuing Mars phase until after the Shmita ended on September 30, then we would have made sense of 2008/early 2009. This would have also allowed us to anticipate the 2015 August crash which happened during a Shmita year.

In 2007, the Dow Jones finished 6.4% despite the credit turmoil afflicting the Housing market. The Dow started the year on momentum from rising above 12000 late in 2006. However, growing concern about the housing crisis dampened investor optimism. Falling housing prices made it difficult for homeowners to refinance their mortgages. Investors shied away from anything related to mortgages. Large investment firms announced billions of dollars in write-downs. Despite these issues, the Dow managed to finish the year positive.

Please note that the Shmita year began September 30, 2007 and lasted until September 30 2008.

In applying the astrological parameters to the year 2007, we see that our bearish indicator began on July 30 2007.

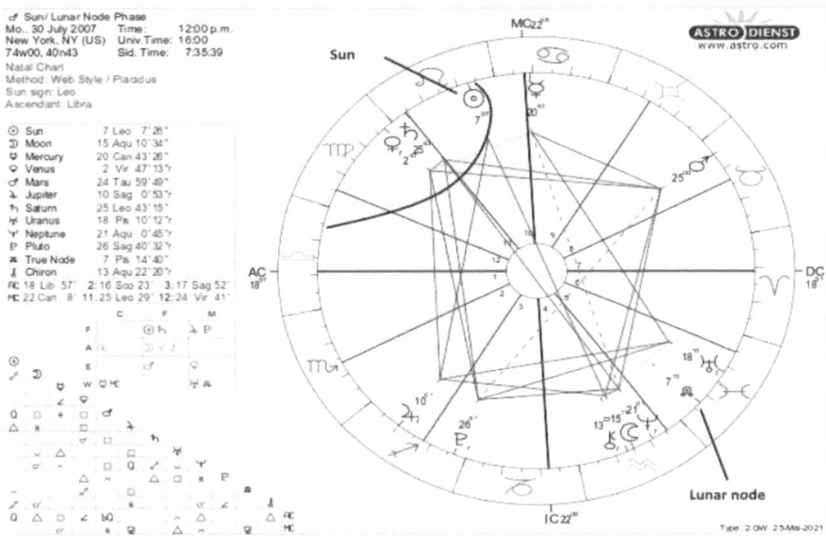

The ensuing Mars phase didn't start until April of 2008 and end the transit there on August 1st 2008. However, we have to be weary of the Shmita year. Theoretically for 2007, we would have projected a bearish outlook from July 30 2007(when the Sun entered within 30 degrees of the lunar node) to August 1st 2008(when the ensuing Mars completed its transit of being within 30 degrees of the lunar node). The Shmita began on September 30, 2007 and would have complicated matters. If we add a rule where the ensuing Mars phase is delayed until after the Shmita year is ended then we would have began our bearish outlook on July 30 2007 and ended it when the next ensuing Mars phase that took place after the Shmita ended finishes its transit of going within 30 degrees of the lunar node. In this case, our bearish prediction would have ended on March 23rd 2009. We could do the same for the Shimta year that took place from September 17, 2000 -September 17, 2001. Our bearish indicator began when the Sun entered within 30 degrees of the lunar node on December 8, 2000. Because its a Shmita year, we have to extend our bearish outlook to last until the next ensuing Mars/lunar node phase that takes place after the Shmita has ended. In this case of 2001 when the Shmita ended on September 17th, the ensuing Mars phase would have completed its transit within 30 degrees of the lunar node on October 26, 2001. This means we would have projected for a bear market to occur between December 8th, 2000 and October 26 2001. This corresponds with what happened during the 2001 recession. From March 14th 2001, the Dow dropped from 9,973.46 to 8,920.70 on September 17, 2001.

Shortly after our bearish indicator occurred on Nov 19 2001, when the Sun re-entered within 30 degrees of the lunar node. It lasted until the ensuing Mars transit within 30 degrees of the lunar node completed on Jun 23 2002. On November 1st 2002, the Sun entered within 30 degrees of the lunar node again. The ensuing Mars transit within 30 degrees of the lunar node took place from December 14, 2002 and lasted until March 9th, just 2 days shy of the actual low point of the Dow Jones decline.

It's important to remember premise behind this thesis is to actively control the market with interest rate setting, as opposed to passive responding. The passive approach is more conducive to inflation.

In 1990, the Dow Jones experienced a recession beginning in July 1990. It lasted until March 1991. The Dow fell 17% in three months from 2,864.60 on August 2nd, 1990 to 2,365.10 on October. 11th 1990 in response to the Iraqi invasion of Kuwait.

On June 29, 1990, the Sun entered with 30 degrees of the lunar node, setting off our bearish outlook. The ensuing Mars phase of Mars being within 30 degrees of the lunar node occurred on March 25th 2001 and lasted until June 26th, 1991. From June 29, 1990 until June 26th 1991, we could have projected a bear market and raised interest rates throughout that time before embarking on a series of cuts after that time period ended.

In 1987, the Dow finished the year the up 2%, but fell 23% on October 19, 1987. Another Smita year had just ended on September 24 1987. The crash was attributed to computer-program trading models that forced sell orders when the market began to drop.

On August 26th 1987, the Sun entered within 30 degrees of the lunar node. Since its during a Shmita year, the ensuing Mars phase becomes delayed until after. On September, 24th, the Shmita year ended. The ensuing Mars phase completed its transit of being within 30 degrees of the lunar node on November 24, 1987. From August 26, 1987 -November 24th, 1987, we would apply a bear market forecast and began raising interest rates. In applying this, we also account for the 23% drop on October 19th.

In 1980, the Dow Jones dropped 16% between February 13th 1980 and April 21st 1980. The Federal Reserve lowered the interest rate in response. It was also another Shmita year September 11, 1979 - September 11, 1980.

On January 19th 1980, the Sun entered within 30 degrees of the lunar node, the start of our bearish projection. Since the ensuing Mars phase is delayed because of the Shmita year, the bearish projection becomes extended. The ensuing Mars phase directly after the Shmita year ended began on December 8th 1980 and lasted until February 20, 1981. From January 19th 1980 - February 20, 1981, we would have forecast for bear market and began raising interest rates during that time. And then cutting them after that time period ended. We would have started raising rates again on December 14, 1981 when the sun entered within 30 degrees of the lunar node. We would have stopped when the ensuing Mars phase of Mars being within 30 degrees of the lunar node ended on December 15th 1982.

Whereas the Federal Reserve actually lowered the funds rate on April 21st 1980, the astrological system would have called for it to be done in February of 1981. Whereas the Federal Reserve raised interest rates after April of 1981, the astrological system would called for it to be done after December of 1981, allowing the market to drop thru December 15th of 1982. In 1982, the Dow hit its low in August of 1982. Therefore its appropriate to surmise that the astrological methodology would have sufficed for purposes of fighting high inflation.

Below is the chart for the Dow Jones from 1980 - 1982. The astrological parameters are applied:

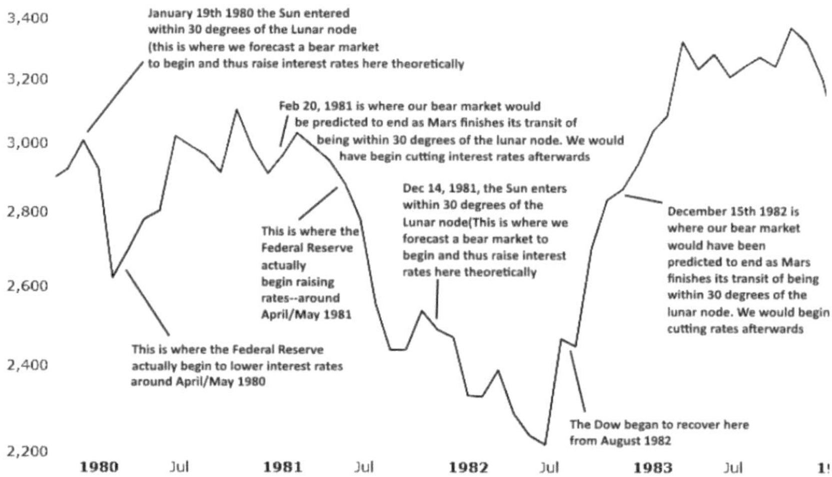

We see in the chart the difference between the Federal Reserve's response approach to setting interest rates(waiting to see what the market does) versus the astrological system's offensive approach to setting interest rates(having it already planned out in advance). The Federal Reserve was about 7-10 months on average ahead of this astrological system in setting their interest rates. 1980-1982 is the perhaps the time period that underscores the importance of dealing with the issue of rising inflation. Throughout the 1970s, rising inflation was largely accepted if it could lead to more jobs. The climax of it in the early 80s has changed how the finance approaches the issue of inflation.

In 1973 and 1974, the Dow Jones was in a recession, due in large part to a steel crisis, the 1973 oil crisis, and the fall of the Bretton Woods system. More nations were becoming industrialized. This triggered more competition in the metals industry. In 1973 OPEC announced an embargo to all nations supporting Israel during the Yom Kippur war. Many of those nations were heavily dependent on oil. In 1971, the US pulled out of the Bretton Woods accord, where the US dollar was pegged to the price of gold, with all other currencies pegged to the dollar. The recession in the US lasted from November of 1973 -March of 1975. On Dec. 4, 1974, the Dow had dropped 45% from its peak of on January. 11, 1973. Please not that there was also another Shmita year in effect from September 27, 1972 -September 27 1973.

On May 28, 1973, the Sun entered within 30 degrees of the lunar node. We would theoretically declare a bear market to start and we also raise interest rates. The ensuing Mars phase within 30 degrees of the lunar node doesn't begin until Feb 20 1974 and lasts until May 22, 1974. So from May, 29, 1973(when the sun went within 30 degrees of the lunar node) all the way until May 22, 1974(when Mars finished its transit of being within 30 degrees of the lunar node), we forsee a bear market and also raise interest rates. When that period has completed, we start lowering interest rates to jump start the economy. Here is the Dow Jones chart for 1973/1974 with the astrological parameters applied.

In 1970, the Dow Jones The Dow dropped 30% between December 3, 1968, and May 26, 1970. US Fiscal tightening in response to their own deficit spending toward the Vietnam war effort had a negative effect on the market.

On August 13, 1969, the Sun entered within 30 degrees of the lunar node. We would theoretically declare a bear market to start there. We also begin raising interest rates. The Ensuing Mars phase began on November 28, 1969 and completed the transit of being within 30 degrees of the lunar node on Feb 8, 1970. Therefore, we would have declared for the bear market to go from August 13, 1969 to Feb 8 1970. See the chart for the Dow Jones in 1969/ 1970 on the next page.

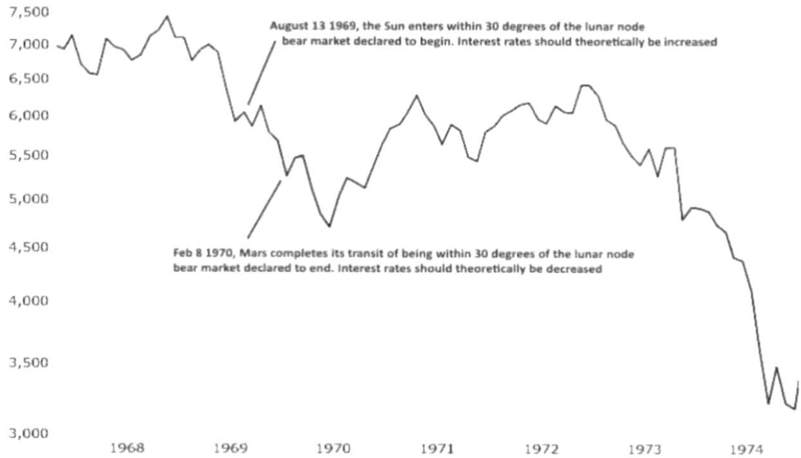

This astrological system missed the low by about 3 months.

In 1962, the US launched a trade embargo against Cuba. The Dow dropped 26% from December 1, 1961 to June 26, 1962. Later in October, it was discovered that the Soviets began shipping ballistic missiles to Cuba. The US demanded for Cuba to remove the missiles and subsequently set up a naval blockade to prevent any ships from reaching Cuba. An agreement was eventually reached between the Soviets and the US, in which the US agreed to remove missiles set in Turkey on the border of the Soviet Union in exchange for the Soviets agreeing to remove their missiles from Cuba.

On January 8th 1962, the Sun entered within 30 degrees of the lunar node. We then theoretically would declare a bear market to begin and start raising interest rates. The ensuing Mars phase of Mars being within 30 degrees of the lunar node was already in motion at this time. It completed the phase on April 2nd 1962. So from January 8th 1962 to April 2nd 1962, the astrological system would have us declare a bear market should occur during that time. See the 1962 chart for the Dow Jones on the next page.

Our astrological-based projections missed the low in 1962 by 2 months.

In 1960, the Dow fell 13% between Dec 31st 1959 and Nov 1st 1960. According to the National Bureau of Economic Research, the recession began in April 1960 and ended in February 1961. The US GDP fell 1.6% during this time. The Federal Reserve began slowly raising interest rates after the recession in 1958 ended, which thus lead to another recession at the start of the 1960s. Arthur Burns, member of the Council of Economic Advisers, warned President Nixon in February of 1960 that a recession was imminent.

Astrologically, we would have theoretically declared in real time that a bear market should begin February 14th 1960, when the Sun entered within 30 degrees of the lunar node. The ensuing Mars phase of Mars being within 30 degrees of the lunar node immediately followed and ended May 3rd 1960.

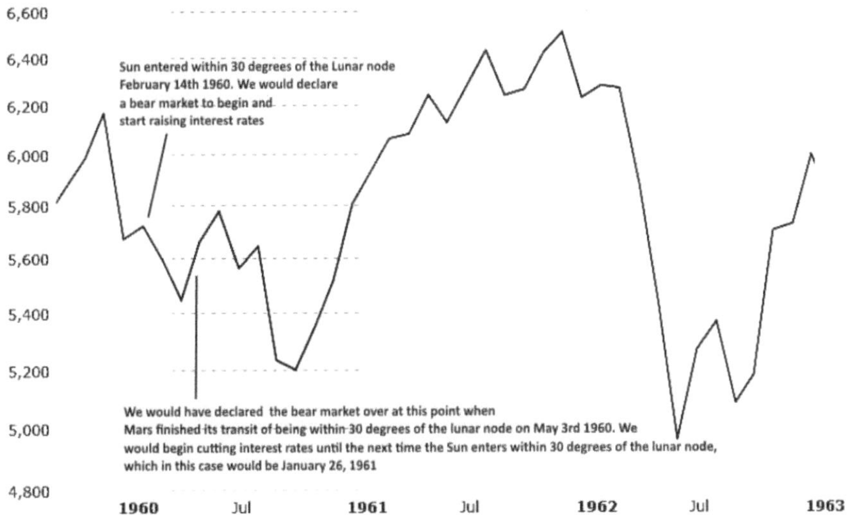

In 1957, the Dow fell 13% between August 1st and November 1st. The Federal Reserve implemented a contractionary monetary policy, resulting in a recession that lasted from August 1957 to April of 1958. The 1957 Asian Flu Pandemic that killed 1 million globally was another factor that hurt the US economy.

On April 10, 1957, the Sun entered within 30 degrees of the lunar node. The ensuing Mars phase of Mars being within 30 degrees of the lunar node was already in motion and completed the phase on April 17, 1957.

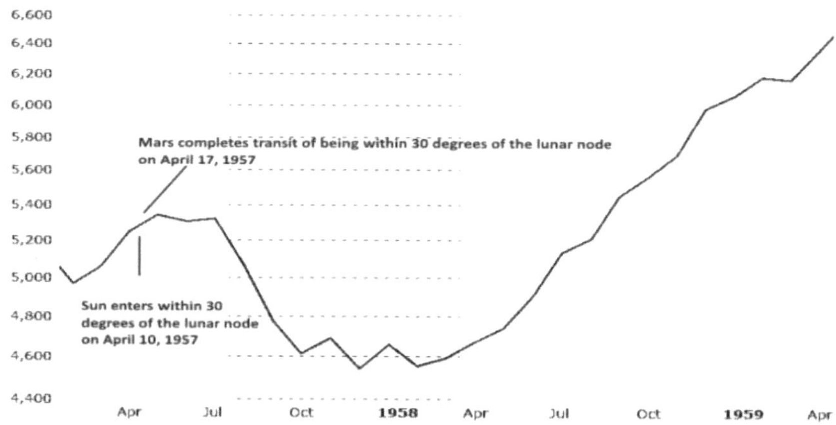

We can see that the low for the year doesn't occur until later in 1957

In 1953, the Dow fell 10% between Jan. 2, 1953 and Sept. 1, 1953. Following the Korean War(1950 - 1953), the US Government reduced its security spending and the Federal Reserve tightened its monetary policies. A 10 month recession took place from July 1953 to May 1954.

On June 25th 1953, the Sun entered within 30 degrees of the lunar node. Mars was within 30 degrees of the lunar node at that time and finished the phase on September 16th, 1953. In the chart on the next page, we see how the parameters aligned with what actually happened in the market. We see the slight dip between the predicted time frame, both in 1953 and 1954. In 1953 the sun entered within 30 degrees of the lunar node on June 25th 1953, while the ensuing Mars phase, which was already in motion ending on September 16, 1953. The market spiked following that period until the nest bear market declaration on June 7th, 1954 when the Sun entered within 30 degrees of the lunar node. This predicted bear market was slated to last until Mars finished its phase of being within 30 degrees of the lunar node on November 3rd 1954.

We see how the astrological system correlated with how the recession was defined to last through September 16th of 1953. And also how a bear market was to last from June -Nov of 1954

The Dow dropped 16% between June 15, 1948 and June 13, 1949 overlapping a recession in which the GDP fell a little less than 2% over an 11 month period between November 1948 and October 1949.

On September 29, 1948, The Sun entered within 30 degrees of the lunar node. The ensuing Mars phase of it being within 30 degrees of the lunar node was already in place and lasted until October 22, 1948. From September 29, 1948 to October 22 1948, we would theoretically declare a bear market to occur during that period and subsequently raise interest rates. We see in the Dow chart how well the system corresponded.

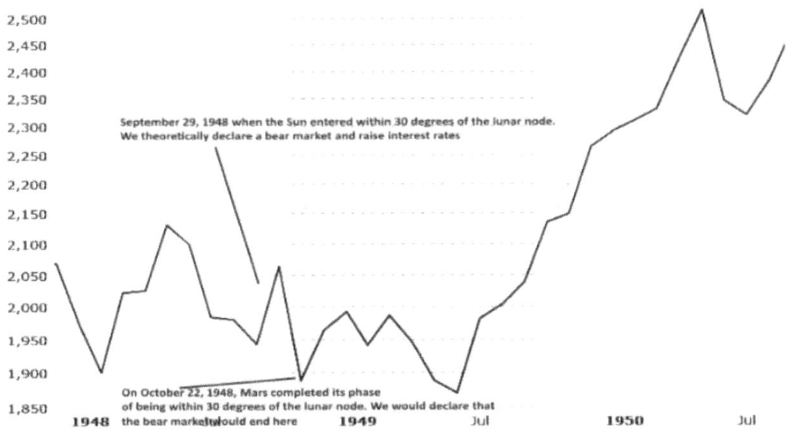

In 1945, the Dow rose 19.2% during a recession that lasted between February and October . The GDP dropped 10.6% as government spending dropped when World War II ended. Business spending, however, increased, which gave a boost to the stock market.

In 1945, the Sun entered within 30 degrees of the lunar node on December 10 1944. The ensuing Mars phase completed its full transit within 30 degrees of the lunar node on March 7th 1945. We would have projected our bear market to last between December 10 1944 and March 7th 1945. Here is the Dow Chart for 1945:

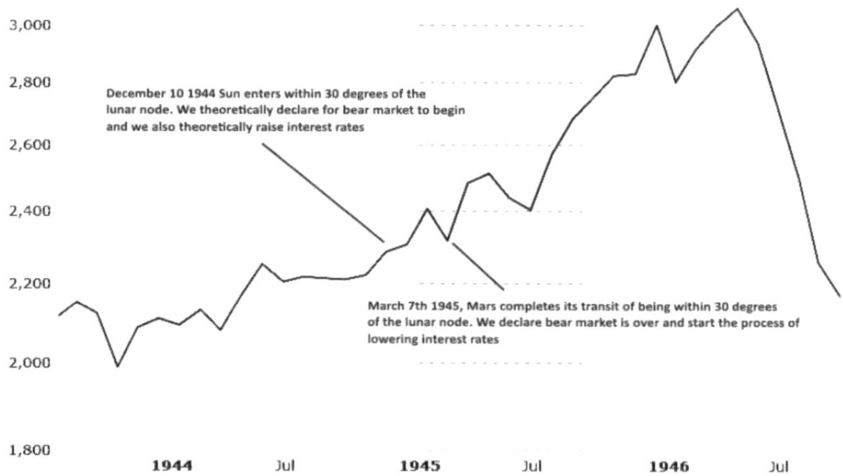

We see how the astrological system applies to the market conditions of 1945.

The Dow experienced another recession between May 1937 and June 1938 as the nation was recovering from the Great Depression. In 1937, President Roosevelt cut Government spending, causing the GDP to fall by 10%.

On May 6th 1937, the Sun entered within 30 degrees of the lunar node. The ensuing Mars phase of Mars being within 30 degrees of the lunar node was already in place and ended on October 11, 1937. Therefore, we would have forecast a bear market to begin on May 6th 1937 and end on October 11, 1937. This falls exactly on the timetable of the actual recession period. See the 1937 Dow Jones Chart on the next page.

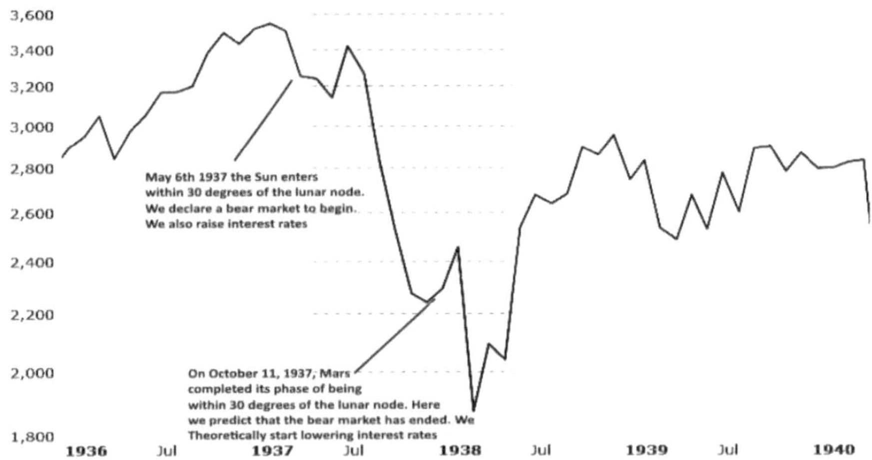

The astrological system applied to 1937/1938 matches up with market conditions

From 1929 - 1932, the Dow Jones fell 90% in what was the beginning of the Great Depression. The stock market crash began on October 24th 1929, Black Thursday and continued until Tuesday of the next week October 29th 1929, Black Tuesday. The 1920s was marked by economic prosperity. It was believed that the market would rise forever. In March of 1929, the Federal Reserve warned of excessive speculation just before a brief slide. Measures taken to curb speculation could be factored in as catalyst for the crash, since speculation played a large role in the market expansion throughout the 1920s. Banks putting deposits in the stock market was considered as another reason for the crash. The Dow reached a bottom on November 13, 1929. The Dow then recovered for several months before peaking on April 17, 1930. The Dow then slid from April 1930 to July 8, 1932. Beginning on March 15, 1933, the Dow began to slowly recover over the remainder of the decade.

On October 6, 1929, the Sun entered within 30 degrees of the Lunar node. Theoretically, we would have declared for a bear market to start and thus began raising interest rates. The ensuing Mars phase began April 27 1930 and completed its transit of being within 30 degrees of the lunar node on July 12, 1930. The Sun re-entered within 30 degrees of the Lunar node on September 18, 1930. The ensuing Mars phase then came on June 29 1931. The Sun however re-entered within 30 degrees of the lunar node on August 29, 1931, which delays the ensuing Mars transit. The ensuing Mars transit starts on February 21 1932 and completes its phase within 30 degrees of the lunar node on May 6th 1932. The next Sun/lunar node phase began August 10 1932. The ensuing Mars/lunar node phase began October 19, 1932. The phase was cut short by Mars retrograde on January 20 1933 and didn't resume until April 13, 1933 and finally completed the phase on July 5th 1933. From this we extrapolate that the astrologically applied series of bear market predictions and interest rate increases since 1929 would have gone as follows:

October 6, 1929 - July 12, 1930
September 18, 1930 -May 6 1932
August 10 1932 -January 20 1933
April 13, 1933 - July 5th 1933

Below are the astrological visuals concerning the application of our parameters for setting the bear market predictions and interest rate increases

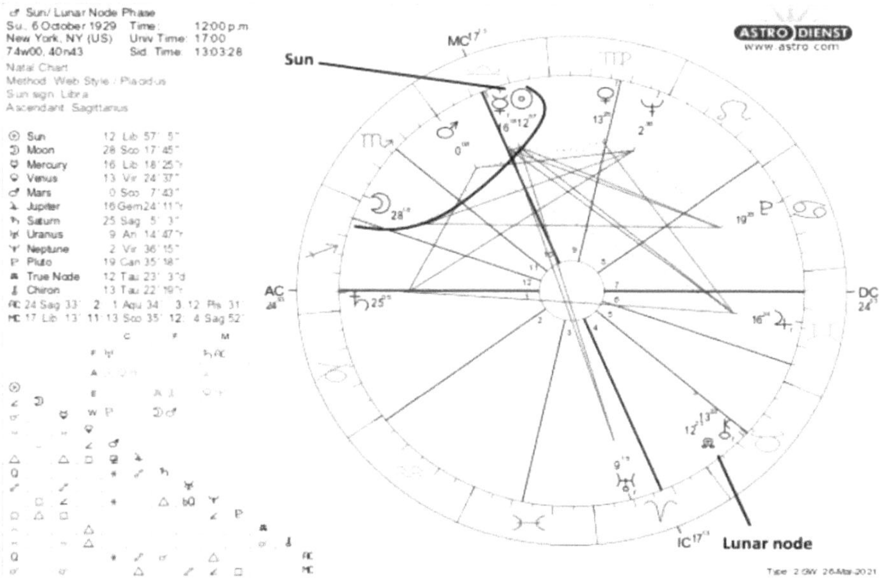

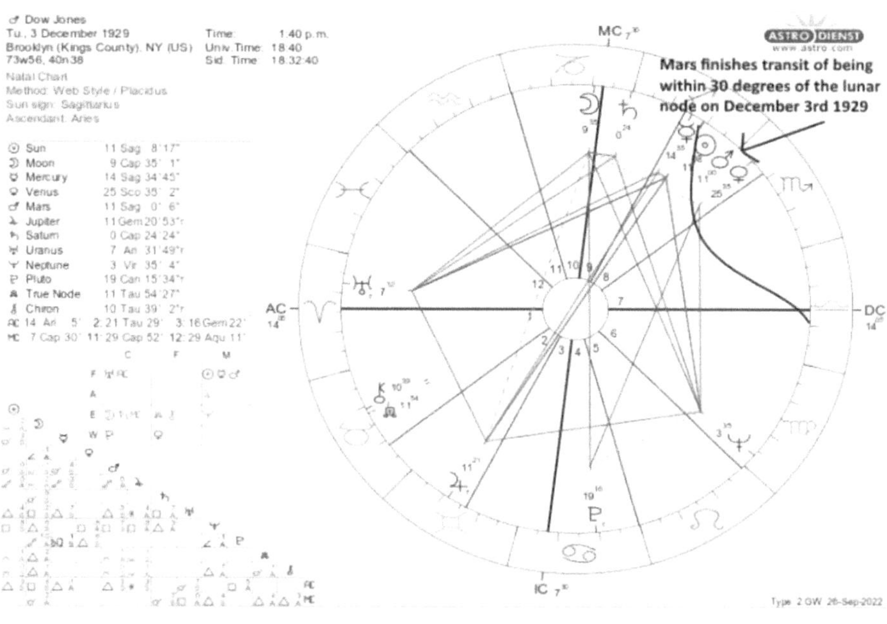

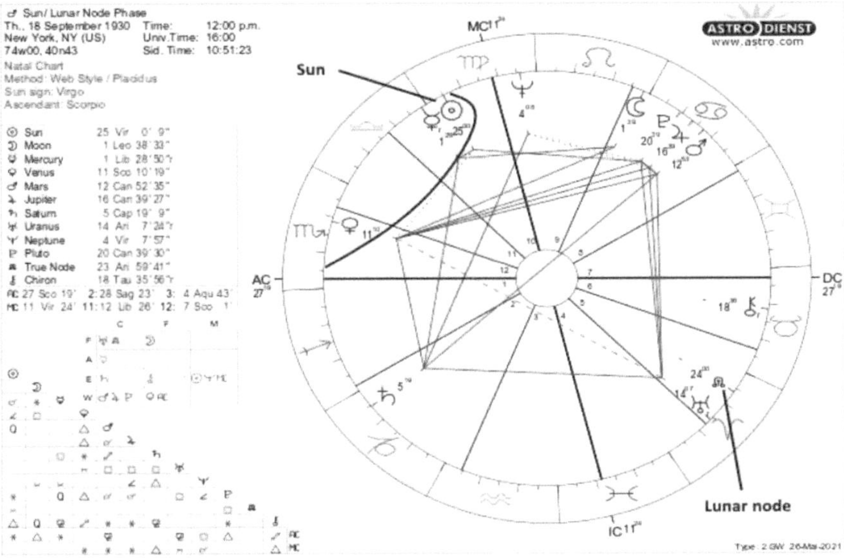
Sun/ Lunar Node Phase
Th., 18 September 1930 Time: 12:00 p.m.
New York, NY (US) Univ.Time: 16:00
74w00, 40n43 Sid. Time: 10:51:23
Natal Chart
Method: Web Style / Placidus
Sun sign: Virgo
Ascendant: Scorpio
Sun 25 Vir 0' 9"
Moon 1 Leo 38' 33"
Mercury 1 Lib 28' 50"r
Venus 11 Sco 10' 19"
Mars 12 Can 52' 35"
Jupiter 16 Can 39' 27"
Saturn 5 Cap 19' 9"
Uranus 14 Ari 7' 24"r
Neptune 4 Vir 7' 57"
Pluto 20 Can 39' 30"
True Node 23 Ari 59' 41"
Chiron 18 Tau 35' 56"r
ASTRO DIENST
www.astro.com
Sun
Lunar node
MC
AC
DC
IC

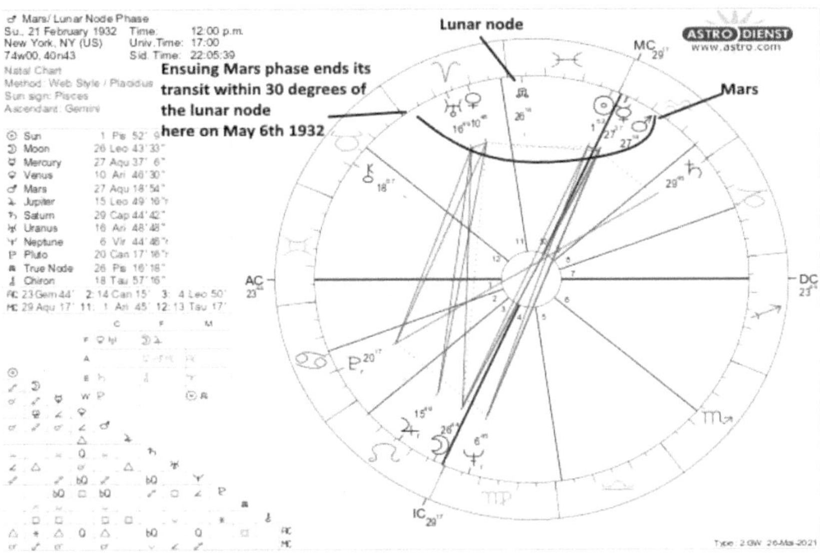
Mars/ Lunar Node Phase
Su., 21 February 1932 Time: 12:00 p.m.
New York, NY (US) Univ.Time: 17:00
74w00, 40n43 Sid. Time: 22:05:39
Natal Chart
Method: Web Style / Placidus
Sun sign: Pisces
Ascendant: Gemini
Sun 1 Pis 52'
Moon 26 Leo 43' 33"
Mercury 27 Aqu 37' 6"
Venus 10 Ari 46' 30"
Mars 27 Aqu 18' 54"
Jupiter 15 Leo 49' 16"r
Saturn 29 Cap 44' 42"
Uranus 16 Ari 48' 48"
Neptune 6 Vir 44' 46"r
Pluto 20 Can 17' 16"r
True Node 26 Pis 16' 18"
Chiron 18 Tau 57' 16"
Lunar node
Ensuing Mars phase ends its transit within 30 degrees of the lunar node here on May 6th 1932
Mars
ASTRO DIENST
www.astro.com
MC
AC
DC
IC

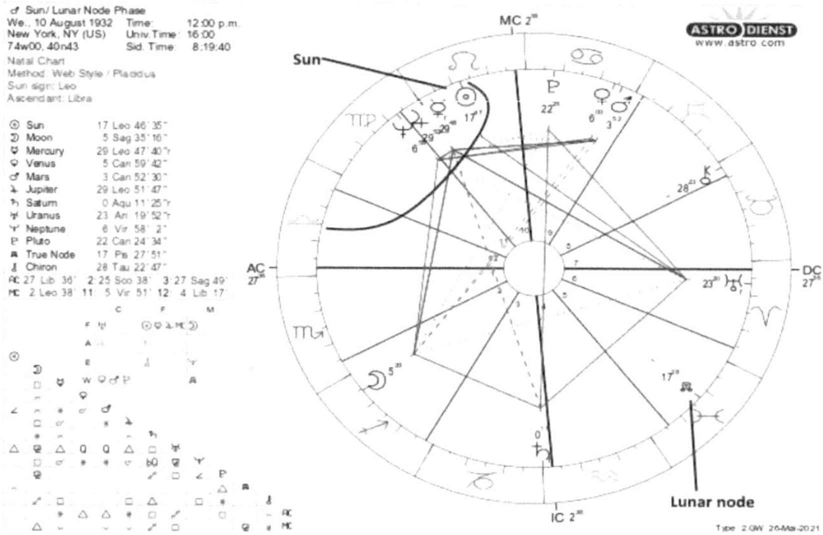
Sun/ Lunar Node Phase
We., 10 August 1932 Time: 12:00 p.m.
New York, NY (US) Univ.Time: 16:00
74w00, 40n43 Sid. Time: 8:19:40
Natal Chart
Method: Web Style / Placidus
Sun sign: Leo
Ascendant: Libra
Sun 17 Leo 46' 35"
Moon 5 Sag 35' 16"
Mercury 29 Leo 47' 40"r
Venus 5 Can 59' 42"
Mars 3 Can 52' 30"
Jupiter 29 Leo 51' 47"
Saturn 0 Aqu 11' 25"r
Uranus 23 Ari 19' 52"r
Neptune 6 Vir 58' 2"
Pluto 22 Can 24' 34"
True Node 17 Pis 27' 51"
Chiron 28 Tau 22' 47"
AC 27 Lib 36' 2: 25 Sco 38' 3: 27 Sag 49'
MC 2 Leo 38' 11: 5 Vir 51' 12: 4 Lib 17'
Sun
Lunar node
MC
AC
DC
IC
ASTRO DIENST
www.astro.com
Type: 2.GW 26-Mai-2021

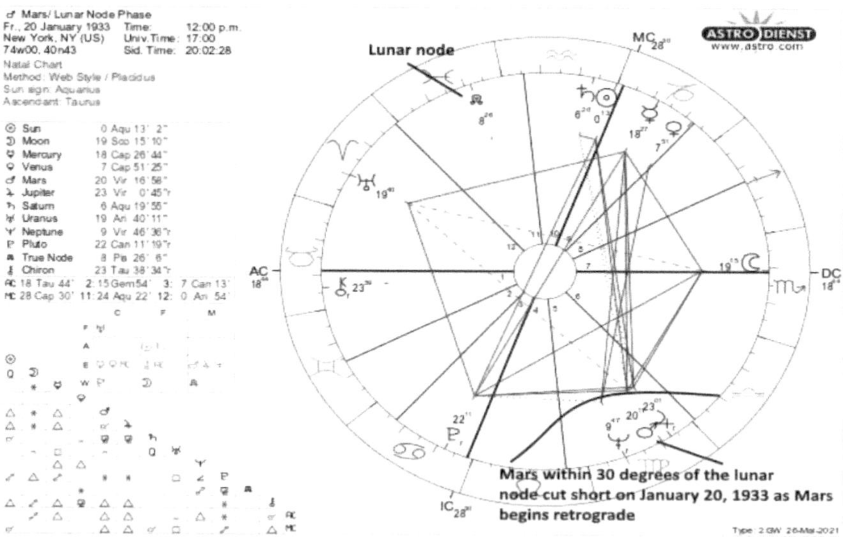
Mars/ Lunar Node Phase
Fr., 20 January 1933 Time: 12:00 p.m.
New York, NY (US) Univ.Time: 17:00
74w00, 40n43 Sid. Time: 20:02:28
Natal Chart
Method: Web Style / Placidus
Sun sign: Aquarius
Ascendant: Taurus
Sun 0 Aqu 13' 2"
Moon 19 Sco 15' 10"
Mercury 18 Cap 26' 44"
Venus 7 Cap 51' 25"
Mars 20 Vir 16' 58"
Jupiter 23 Vir 0' 45"r
Saturn 6 Aqu 19' 55"
Uranus 19 Ari 40' 11"
Neptune 9 Vir 46' 36"r
Pluto 22 Can 11' 19"r
True Node 8 Pis 26' 6"
Chiron 23 Tau 38' 34"r
AC 18 Tau 44' 2: 15 Gem 54' 3: 7 Can 13'
MC 28 Cap 30' 11: 24 Aqu 22' 12: 0 Ari 54'
Lunar node
MC
AC
DC
IC
Mars within 30 degrees of the lunar node cut short on January 20, 1933 as Mars begins retrograde
ASTRO DIENST
www.astro.com
Type: 2.GW 26-Mai-2021

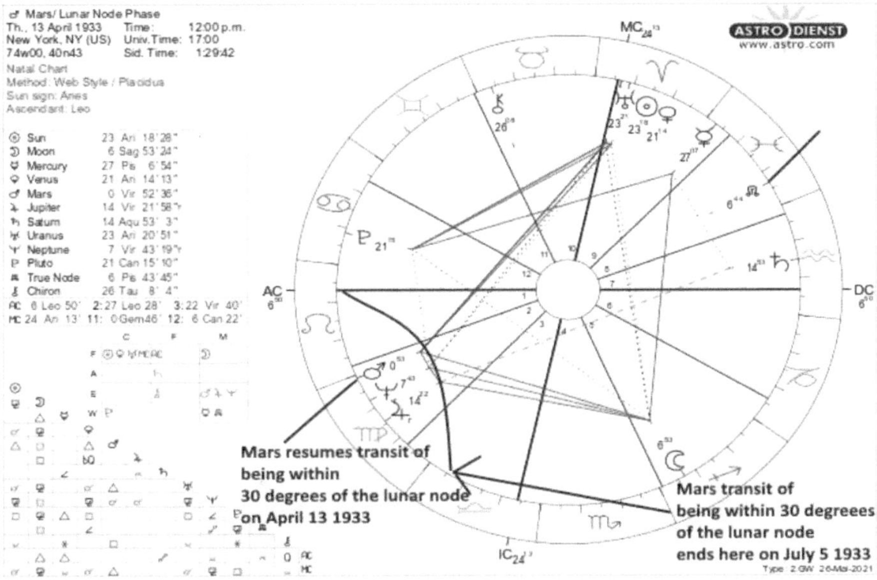

Below is the chart for the Dow Jones between 1929 and 1933 with our astrological parameters applied. We see once again that the astrological parameters applied to the actual market conditions

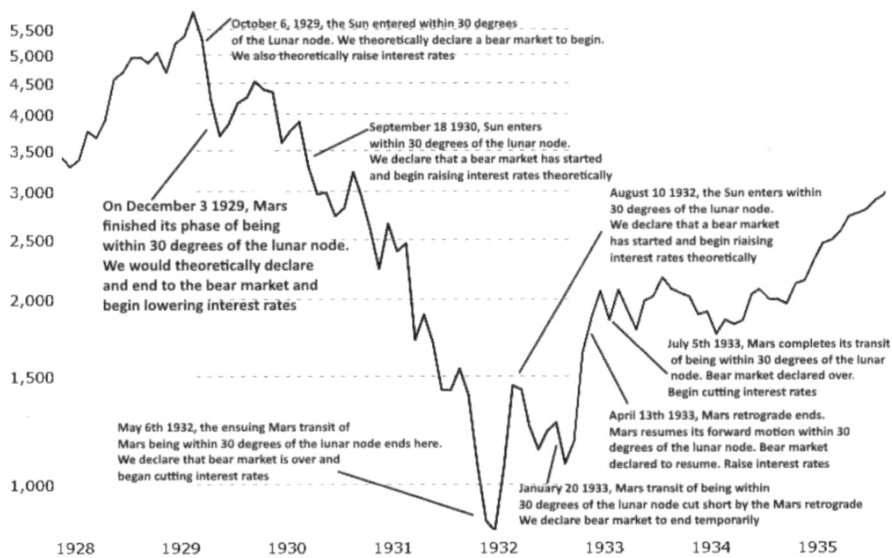

The Bank Panic of 1907 is what led to the creation of the Federal Reserve System and took place between Oct 14, 1907 – Nov 6, 1907. It was triggered by a stock manipulation scheme intended to force short sellers to cover their positions by buying back their borrowed shares. F Augustus Heinz, a mining magnate who owned stock in United Copper Company believed that short sellers were driving down the price of the stock. Together, he, his brother-- broker Otto Heinze, and Wall Street banker Charles W. Morse devised a strategy to force the short sellers to cover their positions and thus create buying pressure that would drive the price of the stock higher. The plan was to aggressively purchase shares of United Copper Company so that the short sellers would have no choice but to buy back their borrowed shares from the Heinzes, who could simply name their price. However, the short sellers were able to find cheaper United Copper Company shares from other sources. This drove the price of the stock down, quickly causing the share price of United Copper Company to collapse. The State Savings bank of Butte, Montana announced its insolvency as they held large stock positions in United Copper Company, which served as collateral against some of their lending. They were also a correspondent bank with the Mercantile National Bank, of which F Augustus Heinze was President. The now tainted reputation of Heinze and his associates as a result of the failed scheme led to a massive bank run in which depositors rushed to withdraw money from Mercantile and other Heinze-associated banks. The panic spread to all financial institutions tied to anyone who was involved in the manipulation scheme. The panic was later brought under control by financier JP Morgan, who put up much of his own money to stabilize the banking system. He also advised other bankers to do the same. The panic underscored the ineffectiveness of the independent Treasury system, which at the time managed the nation's money supply. An investigation of the crisis led to the creation of the Federal Reserve system.

On December 24th, 1906, the Sun entered within 30 degrees of the lunar node. The ensuing Mars phase of Mars being within 30 degrees of the lunar node began March 30 1907 and was cut short by the Mars retrograde that began on June 5th. Therefore a bear market would have been declared to occur between December 24, 1906 and June 5th 1907(we also theoretically raise interest rates at this time). The bear market would have been declared to resume when the Mars retrograde phase ended on August 8 1907 and then declared to finally end on November 8 1907 when Mars finished its transit of being within 30 degrees of the lunar node. On the next page is the chart for the stock market in 1907 and the astrological parameters applied.

We see once again that the astrological parameters applied to the actual market conditions in 1907.

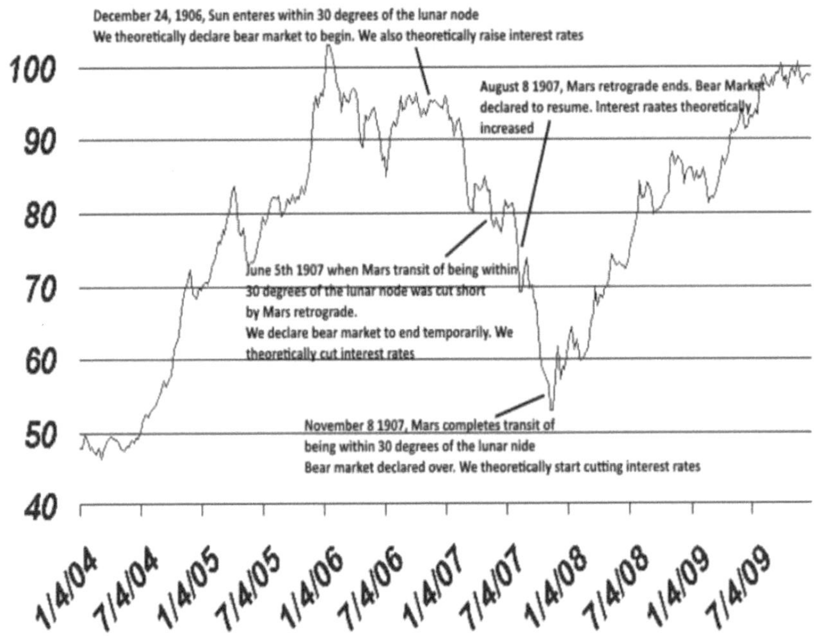

JayHenry at English Wikipedia

Throughout the course of this demonstration of applying astrological factors in order to make the case that the Federal Reserve can set interest rates based on the position of the planet Mars, we saw how the parameters applied in some cases and not others. Adding the Shmita year to the equation helped significantly make sense of how the algorithm seemed to be going way off course every 7 years. Now, I will extrapolate the algorithm rules and apply the parameters for future predictions. The basic idea is that when the Sun enters within 30 degrees of the lunar node(on the opposite side of the actual position of the lunar node as presented earlier in the writing), a bear market should be declared; interest rates should be increased. The ensuing Mars phase of which Mars is within 30 degrees of the lunar node(Mars can be within 30 degrees of the lunar node on either side of the lunar node position--opposite or conjunct) and completes the transit should mark the end of the bear market; interest rates should be decreased.

The Shmita years are 1909-1910, 1916-1917, 1923-1924, 1930-1931, 1937-1938, 1944-1945, 1951-1952 1958–1959, 1965–1966, 1972–1973, 1979–1980, 1986–1987, 1993–1994, 2000–2001, 2007–2008, 2014–2015, 2021-2022, 2028-2029 etc. They are usually every seven years starting September and end in September the next year. This algorithm posits that the market will simply drop during those times.

Keep in mind that Mars within 30 degrees of the lunar node can be on either side of the position of the lunar node--conjunct or opposite.) If after Mars's entry within 30 degrees of the lunar node, Mars itself goes retrograde, then the bear market is declared over(interest rates are cut). When the Mars retrograde ends, the bear market is declared to be resumed(interest rates are increased) if Mars is still within 30 degrees of the lunar node. If it is, when it finishes the transit of being within 30 degrees of the lunar node, the bear market can then be declared over; interest rates can be decreased.

Based on those parameters, I will set up the astrological-based market projections for the future, and also the interest rate setting recommendations.

Here are some future dates of bear markets. Be sure to raise interest rates at the start of the bear market, and lower interest rates after the bear market ends

October 24 2021 - January 24, 2022
(Shmita year Sept 2021-Sept 2022)
October 6, 2022 -January 24, 2023
September 19, 2023 - Nov 15, 2023
August 30 2024 - September 4, 2025
July 24, 2026 - June 16, 2027
July 3 2027 - February 12 2028
June 14 2028 - October 5 2028
(Shmita year Sept 2028-Sept 2029)
May 26 2029 -December 7 2029
May 7 2030 - July 22 2030
April 18 2031 - September 27 2031

April 1 2032 - May 12 2032
March 13, 2033 - March 2, 2034
February 4 2035 - December 1 2035
(Shmita year Sept 2035-Sept 2036)
January 17 2036 -September 2 2036
December 29 2036 - April 28 2037
December 11 2037 - June 15 2038
November 23 2038 - February 20 2039
November 6 2039 -March 11, 2040
October 18 2040 -December 13 2040
October 1 2041 - October 4 2042
(Shmita year Sept 2042-Sept 2043)

Here is how "The Mars Hypothesis" works. Basically, the Federal Reserve can set interest rates based on the movements of the planet Mars. That hypothesis is constructed into form by taking past bear market cycles and correlating them to the position of Mars. A calendar based on the position of the Sun is then applied and is to serve as the fiscal calendar for the Federal Reserve. The first day of when the Sun enters within 30 degrees of the lunar node is to serve as the first day of the fiscal year. That is also when a bear market should be projected by the Fed. From that point, the Fed would raise interest rates. This would continue until the ensuing Mars phase finishes its phase of being within 30 degrees of the lunar node.(Sometimes the ensuing Mars phase takes a while to occur, hence why some bear markets last longer than others). This book hypothesizes that the low of the projected bear market should occur within the time frame of that ensuing Mars phase(Mars within 30 degrees of the lunar node). After that ensuing Mars phase ends, the Fed would begin to cut rates until the start of the next fiscal year.

The next start of the Fed fiscal year is October 24, 2021(Sun enters within 30 degrees of the lunar node.) The ensuing Mars phase of Mars being within 30 degrees of the lunar node begins on November 4, 2021 and last until January 24, 2022. So basically, the Fed should project a bear market to take place from October 24, 2021 to January 24, 2022 and should raise interest within that time. In real time, The market dropped between October 24, 2021 and January 24, 2022. Notice that between September 2021 and September 2022 is a Shmita year. So hence we can expect the market to decline the entire year, which it did, dropping around 18%.

The next dates are between October 6, 2022 and January 24, 2023. The Sun enters within 30 degrees of the lunar node on October 6th 2022. At this time, Mars is already within 30 degrees of the lunar node and will complete that phase on January 24, 2023. However between October 30 2022 and January 12, 2023, Mars will be retrograde. Mars enters within 30 degrees of the lunar node while retrograde on December 26, 2022 which means that within the predicted bear market phase between October 6, 2022 and January 24, 2023, the fed would theoretically anticipate a bull market to occur during the mars retrograde period between December 26 2022 and January 12, 2023 and thus lower interest rates. When Mars goes direct on January 13th, 2023, it remains within 30 degrees of the lunar node until January 24, 2022. During that time, interest rates should be raised. After the completion, however, interest rates should be lowered again. Keep in mind that when Mars is within 30 degrees of the lunar while retrograde, we do not count that as a negative influence derived from being within 30 degrees of the lunar node.

After that bear market forecast, the next forecast is to anticipate a bear market to last between September 19th 2023 and November 15th 2023. On September 19th 2023, the Sun enters within 30 degrees of the lunar node and on November 15th, 2023, Mars completes its phase of being within 30 degrees of the lunar node. During that time, a bear market should be expected and interest rates should be raised.

The next bear market prediction timeframe is between August 30, 2024 and September 4, 2025. On August 30th, 2024, the Sun enters within 30 degrees of the lunar node, setting off the start of the projected bear market. On September 4th 2025, the ensuing Mars phase finishes its transit within 30 degrees of the lunar node, ending out predicted bear market timeframe.

The next predicted bear market phase is between July 24, 2026 - June 16, 2027. On July 24, 2026, the Sun enters within 30 degrees of the lunar node, starting our bear market projection. Mars finishes its ensuing transit of being within 30 degrees of the lunar node on June 16, 2027. However, keep in mind that between the time frame of July 24, 2026 - June 16, 2027, Mars, while its within 30 degrees of the lunar node, will be retrograde between January 10, 2027 and April 1, 2027. Be sure to predict a bull market and cut interest rates during that retrograde time. After Mars retrograde ends on April 1st 2027, we anticipate a market decline until Mars finishes its transit within 30 degrees of the lunar node on June 16, 2027. After that we predict the bear market to end there and we subsequently began lowering interest rates. The rest of the predicted bear market dates are self explanatory, however, one must keep watch over the Mars retrogrades that occur while

Mars is within 30 degrees of the lunar node. Here is the list of Mars retrograde dates while the ensuing Mars phase is within 30 degrees of the lunar node:

March 28th 2031 - June 13, 2031 August 15, 2035 - October 15, 2035 January 4th, 2040 - February 9 2040

Keep these dates. Mars retrograde dates as well as the aforementioned ones in mind when reading the list of dates that project a bear market.

Sources

Planet Watcher - Current Transiting Positions in Astrology planetwatcher.com

How to Short a Stock | The Motley Fool www.fool.com

The Fed Was Born As a Result of This 'Panic' www.businessinsider.com

Dow Jones - DJIA - 100 Year Historical Chart | MacroTrends www.macrotrends.net

Dow Jones History: Top Highs and Lows Since 1929 www.thebalance.com

Wall Street Crash of 1929 - Wikipedia en.wikipedia.org

What happened in every U.S. recession since the Great Depression www.cnbc.com

USA History - Recession of 1960 www.globalsecurity.org

Recession of 1960–1961 - Wikipedia en.wikipedia.org

Ares Le Mandat 7th Edition by Anthony Moore (Anthony of Boston) :: SSRN papers.ssrn.com

1973–1975 recession - Wikipedia en.wikipedia.org

1973 oil crisis - Wikipedia en.wikipedia.org

Gauquelin, M. (1988). Is there really a Mars effect? Above & Below: Journal of Astrological Studies, 11(Fall) pp. 4-7

SKEPTICAL INQUIRER, Vol. 16 Update on the "Mars Effect" by SUITBERT ERTEL

The Dow's Biggest One-Day Drops

Here's where yesterday's drop of 586 points ranks among the worst drops in the Dow's history:

Date	Close	Change	Percent
9/29/2008	10,365.45	-777.68	-6.98%
10/15/2008	8,577.91	-733.08	-7.87%
9/17/2001	8,920.70	-684.81	-7.13%
12/1/2008	8,149.09	-679.95	-7.70%
10/9/2008	8,579.19	-678.92	-7.33%
8/8/2011	10,809.85	-634.76	-5.55%
4/14/2000	10,305.78	-617.78	-5.66%
8/24/2015	15,873.22	-586.53	-3.56%
10/27/1997	7,161.14	-554.26	-7.18%
8/21/2015	16,459.75	-530.94	-3.12%

Largest daily percentage losses[5]

Rank	Date	Close	Change	
			Net	%
1	1987-10-19	1,738.74	−508.00	−22.61
2	2020-03-16	20,188.52	−2,997.10	−12.93
3	1929-10-28	260.64	−38.33	−12.82
4	1929-10-29	230.07	−30.57	−11.73
5	2020-03-12	21,200.62	−2,352.60	−9.99
6	1929-11-06	232.13	−25.55	−9.92
7	1899-12-18	58.27	−5.57	−8.72
8	1932-08-12	63.11	−5.79	−8.40
9	1907-03-14	76.23	−6.89	−8.29
10	1987-10-26	1,793.93	−156.83	−8.04
11	2008-10-15	8,577.91	−733.08	−7.87
12	1933-07-21	88.71	−7.55	−7.84
13	2020-03-09	23,851.02	−2,013.76	−7.79
14	1937-10-18	125.73	−10.57	−7.75
15	2008-12-01	8,149.09	−679.95	−7.70
16	2008-10-09	8,579.19	−678.91	−7.33
17	1917-02-01	88.52	−6.91	−7.24
18	1997-10-27	7,161.14	−554.26	−7.18
19	1932-10-05	66.07	−5.09	−7.15
20	2001-09-17	8,920.70	−684.81	−7.13

www.ingramcontent.com/pod-product-compliance
Lightning Source LLC
LaVergne TN
LVHW051136210926
848482LV00006B/331